Mike Storms
PARENTING 101
PARENT'S WORKBOOK
A PRACTICAL HANDS-ON GUIDE TO RAISING REMARKABLE KIDS

MICHAEL B. STORMS

PRESS LLC

SANFORD • FLORIDA

Scripture quotations marked AMP are taken from the AMPLIFIED® Bible. Copyright © 1954, 1958, 1962, 1964, 1965, 1987 by The Lockman Foundation. Used by permission. (www.Lockman.org)

Scripture quotations marked KJV are from The Holy Bible, KING JAMESVERSION. Copyright © 1970 by Thomas Nelson Inc.

Scripture quotations marked NASB are taken from the NEW AMERICANSTANDARD BIBLE®. Copyright © 1960, 1962, 1963, 1968, 1971, 1972, 1973, 1975, 1977, 1995 by The Lockman Foundation. Used by permission. (www.Lockman.org)

Scripture quotations marked NIV are taken from the HOLY BIBLE, NEWINTERNATIONAL VERSION®. Copyright ©1973, 1978, 1984 Biblica. Used by permission of Zondervan. All rights reserved.

The "NIV" and "New International Version" trademarks are registered in the United States Patent and Trademark Office by Biblica. Use of either trade-mark requires the permission of Biblica.

Scripture quotations marked NKJV are taken from the NEW KING JAMES VERSION. Copyright © 1982 by Thomas Nelson, Inc. Used by permission. All rights reserved.

Scripture quotations marked NLT are taken from the Holy Bible, NEWLIVING TRANSLATION, copyright © 1996, 2004. Used by permission of Tyndale House Publishers, Inc., Wheaton, IL 60189. All rights reserved.

Scripture quotations marked The Message are taken from THE MESSAGE. Copyright © 1993, 1994, 1995, 1996, 2000, 2001, 2002. Used by permission of Nav Press Publishing Group.

Scripture quotations marked TLB are taken from THE LIVING BIBLE. Copyright © 1971 by Tyndale House Publishers, Wheaton, IL60187. All rights reserved.

Unless otherwise noted, italics and bold treatment used in Scriptures and quotes indicate the author's added emphasis.

EDITOR AND CONCEPT DEVELOPMENT:

Vincent M. Newfield v New Fields & Company v P.O. Box 622 v Hillsboro, Missouri 63050 v www.preparethewaytoday.org

TEXT DESIGN: Lisa Simpson www.simpsonproductions.net
COVER DESIGN: Stephanie Katz

ISBN: 978-1-932021-58-5
Printed in USA
10 9 8 7 6 5 4 3 2

Contents

Before You Begin...

Welcome to *Mike Storms Parenting 101 Workbook*! It is a privilege to present to you this practical, rubber-meets-the-road study on how to raise wonderful kids. It is the companion to both the book and the CD teaching series. Much prayer, study, and research have been poured into the pages of the book you now hold in your hands. We firmly believe that as you seek God and work through each lesson, you will learn things about your children, yourself, and God that you have never seen before—truths that will transform the way you parent and enhance the quality of your family life.

In this study you will discover eight chapters that correspond to the eight CD sessions and the chapters in the *Parenting 101* book. It includes a series of soul-searching questions, true stories, as well as an area to jot down notes and take *Time to Reflect* on what you learn in each lesson. The other elements you will find in each chapter include...

- AGELESS ADVICE – timeless truth from God's Word that will transform your life

- A PAGE FROM THE PLAYBOOK – eye-opening insights from fellow fathers and mothers and godly leaders that help drive home the heart of the message

- SENSEI SAYS – powerful points I made in the book and CD sessions that emphasize the important principles worth remembering

- SOMETHING TO THINK ABOUT – interesting facts and information that tie into the topic at hand

Take your time as you journey through this study—don't rush. If there is something you don't understand, it's okay. Put it "on the shelf" and pray for God to give you the ability to comprehend what He is trying to teach you. Again, write down any special insights the Lord reveals to you along the way. What He speaks to your heart is priceless and well worth investing the time to write.

We Also Suggest That You...

- START AND END EACH LESSON WITH PRAYER. Invite God's Spirit to teach you and guide you into all truth (see John 16:13). As you finish, ask Him to take the things you have learned and permanently seal them in your heart.

- READ THE CHAPTERS IN THE BOOK AND LISTEN TO THE CD TEACHINGS and then complete the lesson in the workbook.

- PACE YOURSELF to finish each lesson in a timely manner. You may do it as part of your daily routine or work on it a few nights a week. There is no right or wrong way to do it; it is your *personal* study with the Lord.

- BE CONSISTENT. Decide on a time and place to do your study, and stick to it. If you fall behind, don't quit. *Keep going* to the end. God will bless your every effort.

- BE HONEST with yourself and God as you answer each question. Knowing the truth of God's Word and the truth about yourself will bring freedom to your life that can be found no other way.

God loves you, my friend! He wants to heal any hurts you have received while growing up and keep them from being passed on to your children. He is the perfect parent who desires to show you things that will bring great peace and fulfillment to you and your family. Take a moment now to surrender yourself to Him in prayer. Say...

"Lord, here I am. Thank You for this study. I give myself to You. I surrender all my fears and misconceptions of parenting. Teach me. Show me clearly how to parent my children and enjoy the time You have given me with them. I believe when I am finished with this study, I will not be the same person I am right now. I trust You to change me. In Jesus' name, Amen."

Chapter 1

Understanding How Your Kids Are Shaped

"Our most effective teaching tool is our own behavior —how we ourselves live and treat others. When virtue is manifest in us, we plant the seeds of love and good manners in our children's hearts. The examples we set for our children are profoundly important for their moral formation. Our children do not need to know that we are perfect, because none of us are; rather, they simply need to know that we too are trying to live decent and respectable lives, treating others by the Golden Rule: 'Do unto others as you would have them do to you' (Luke 6:31)."

—Karen Santorum[1]

Chapter 1

Understanding How Your Kids Are Shaped

Please refer to Chapter 1 in the *Parenting 101* book along with Session 1 of the CD series.

SENSEI SAYS...

"Raising excellent, happy, healthy, confident kids is our goal, right? So what makes kids nice to be around? What makes them happy, cheerful, successful, and responsible teens? In contrast, what makes them weak, whiny, excuse-making failures that no one wants to be around? I've had the opportunity to work with over 5,000 kids and many of their parents. I have experience in what works and what doesn't work, and I want to share those things with you."

—**Mike Storms**

(1) One of the strongest influences that determines how our children are shaped is the *media* they consume. What goes in is what comes out. Input equals output. By God's grace you can learn how to monitor your kids' "media menu."

(a) Put these media menu items in order of importance for each of your children:

Movies • Music • Magazines • Books • Video Games

Child 1 _____ _____

Child 2 _____ _____

Child 3 _____ _____

Knowing what is most important to them will help you know what requires greatest monitoring and what to take away when their behavior needs to improve.

(b) About how many hours a day/week do your children spend doing the following:

MEDIA TYPE	CHILD 1:	CHILD 2:	CHILD 3:
Watching TV (Movies, Cable, etc.)			
Listening to Music (MP3, IPOD, Radio, etc.)			
Playing Video Games			

(c) What type of movies, music, video games, etc., are your kids feeding on?

_____

_____

_____

If you don't know the answers to these questions, venture into their world and find out.

TRUE STORY:

"INPUT = OUTPUT"

If you ever doubt the truth of this equation or statement, answer this question for yourself: If you, or your kids, watch a scary movie before going to bed, what usually happens that night? You guessed it—there is a pretty good chance that nightmares will occur. The truth of the matter is that all input, negative and positive, must show up in behavior sooner or later. It has to.

I remember when I was a kid, I used to watch Tom and Jerry, the cat and mouse cartoon. There was a scene in one of the shows where Jerry, the mouse, hid behind a corner, stood on a chair, and hit Tom over the head with a heavy object. I thought that was really clever. Well, I have a sister who is two years older than me, and we used to share a room when we were little. When I was about four, I decided to reenact the scene from Tom and Jerry. I got up on my dresser, held one of my stuffed animals with a hard plastic head that talked when you pulled the string, and when my sister walked in the room, "WHAM!" Now, my mom gave me some good discipline that night, and my dad threw the doll into the garbage.

Clearly, input = output. I know firsthand that this happens. Years ago, I saw my own kids watch a TV show with a rude, or sassy child and then they imitated him. My point is, guard against negative inputs—eliminate them as much as possible. When you do, it will be much easier to produce the excellent, kind, respectful children you desire.

SOMETHING TO THINK ABOUT

"It is time to recognize that the true tutors of our children are not school teachers or university professors but filmmakers, advertising executives, and pop culture purveyors. Disney does more than Duke, Spielberg outweighs Stanford, MTV trumps MIT."

—**University of Maryland Professor**[2]

(2) The younger our children are, the more control is needed over the *quality* and *quantity* of media they are consuming. As they mature, we can teach them how to choose for themselves entertainment that has redeeming value and does not dishonor God. In light of your answers from question one:

(a) Can you see any connection between your children's behavior and what they're watching and listening to? What is it?

_____

_____

_____

(b) Are there any specific movies, CDs, etc., that you feel it is best to get rid of?

_____

_____

_____

SENSEI SAYS...

"TV influences your behavior and turns you into a consumer. It makes you discontented with your looks, your clothes, your possessions, your house, your spouse, etc. Stay away from evil influences in the media; they will be counterproductive to good parenting."

—**Mike Storms**

AGELESS ADVICE

"*Guard your heart* above all else, for it determines the course of your life."

—**Proverbs 4:23 NLT**

(3) When it comes to guarding our kids' heart, we can't just eliminate the negative. We must also present them with positive alternatives. There is no greater source of "soul" food than the timeless truth of God's Word.

(a) Carefully *read* these Bible verses and *write* the benefits you and your children will receive from feasting on the fabulous food of God's Word.

JOSHUA 1:8 AND PSALM 1:1-3

_____

_____

_____

PSALM 19:8 AND JEREMIAH 15:16

_____

_____

_____

ROMANS 15:4 AND 2 TIMOTHY 3:16,17

_____

_____

_____

(b) Do your children have Bibles that they understand? How about you?

_____

_____

Two easy-to-read versions of the Bible to consider include the New International Version (NIV) and the New Living Translation (NLT).

The next best thing to giving your kids God's Word is giving them media that is filled with His Word. Thankfully, there are many godly options for you to choose from. Check out some healthy "Media Menu" options located in Appendix A of the workbook.

SENSEI SAYS...

"You can't expect your kids to respect you if they are watching disrespectful behavior being presented on television and in movies as 'funny.' Likewise, you can't let your kids hang out with kids who curse and get bad grades and not expect them to do the same thing. You have to be the policeman over what their input is—what they listen to, what they watch, and who they hang out with."

—Mike Storms

AGELESS ADVICE

"How can a young man keep his way pure? By living according to your word."

—Psalm 119:9 NIV

(4) Another major influence that shapes our children's behavior is *peer pressure*. Clearly, who they hang out with is going to have a definite degree of influence on their habits, language, dress, and overall level of success.

(a) Looking back on your life, what friends made a *positive* impact on you? Who made a *negative* impact? How does this knowledge influence you with your kids?

_____

_____

_____

(b) Who are your kids hanging out with that has a positive influence on their lives? What can you do to encourage and strengthen these relationships?

_____

_____

_____

(5) Who your children associate with becomes increasingly important as they get older. Take a moment to assess your children's closest friends by answering the following questions.

PAL APPRAISAL

How do your kids' friends measure up?

- How do they treat and talk to/about their parents?

_____

- How do they treat their siblings?

_____

- How do they act toward people in authority?

_____

- What kind of grades do they make in school?

_____

- What are their interests, hobbies, and goals in life?

_____

- Do they challenge your children to do good *or* motivate them to be mischievous?

_____

- What is their attitude toward God?

_____

You may have to do a little investigating to find out the answers to these questions, but it's well worth knowing. If your children are spending a lot of time with one or more kids who are a negative influence, don't verbally assassinate them in your children's ears. Calmly and confidently point out some of the problems you foresee if they continue to associate with them. Then help your son or daughter find friends who are headed in the right direction—kids with common interests, values, and goals that you want your children to imitate.

A PAGE FROM THE PLAYBOOK

"The Scriptures speak very plainly about the dangers of conformity. God in His wisdom knew that social pressure could keep us from doing what is right, and He spoke strongly against it. ...God does not want us to follow the whims of the world around us. He expects us to say to ourselves, 'I am going to control my behavior, my mind, my body, and my life. I will be like my friends in ways that *don't* matter, such as wearing fashionable clothes when convenient. But when it comes to being moral and obeying God and learning in school and keeping my body clean and healthy, then I won't let anybody tell me what to do. If they must laugh at me, then let them laugh. The joke won't be funny for very long."

—Dr. James Dobson[3]

AGELESS ADVICE

"Do not be conformed to this world (this age), [fashioned after and adapted to its external, superficial customs], but be transformed (changed) by the [entire] renewal of your mind [by its new ideals and its new attitude], so that you may prove [for yourselves] what is the good and acceptable and perfect will of God, even the thing which is good and acceptable and perfect [in His sight for you]."

—Romans 12:2 AMP

(6) The Bible has some clear-cut things to say about the company we, and our kids, keep. Carefully *read* the selected

scriptures, and **write** what God is revealing to you and how it relates to helping your children choose good friends.

"Become wise by walking with the wise; hang out with fools and watch your life fall to pieces."
                                    —Proverbs 13:20 The Message

"Do not be misled: "Bad company corrupts good character."
                                    —1 Corinthians 15:33 NIV

_____

_____

_____

"Don't do as the wicked do, and don't follow the path of evildoers. Don't even think about it; don't go that way. Turn away and keep moving."
                                    —Proverbs 4:14,15 NLT

"Don't envy evil people or desire their company. For their hearts plot violence, and their words always stir up trouble."
                                    —Proverbs 24:1,2 NLT

_____

_____

_____

"Make no friendship with an angry man, and with a furious man do not go, lest you learn his ways and set a snare for your soul."
                                    —Proverbs 22:24,25 NKJV

_____

_____

_____

"Do not be unequally yoked with unbelievers [do not make mismated alliances with them or come under a different yoke with them, inconsistent with your faith]. For what partnership have right living and right standing with God with iniquity and lawlessness? Or how can light have fellowship with darkness?"

—2 Corinthians 6:14 AMP

_____

_____

_____

SENSEI SAYS...

"Show me your friends and I will show you your future. Take charge of who your kids associate with. If you don't approve of them, they can't hang out with them."

—Mike Storms

SOMETHING TO THINK ABOUT

"A farmer once went to the county fair with a pumpkin that was the exact size and shape of a two-gallon jug. His pumpkin won the blue ribbon. When someone asked how he got a pumpkin to look like that, he said, 'It was easy. As soon as it started to grow, I stuck it inside a two-gallon jug.' Paul exhorts us to not be conformed to this world (Romans 12:2). If we don't heed his advice, we will soon find ourselves pressed into the mold of this world."[4]

(7) The third major factor that determines the shape and quality of your kids is *you*. Your correction, direction, and overall involvement in your children's lives will powerfully impact and shape the grown-ups they become.

(a) On a scale of 1 to 10, how would you rate yourself as a parent? How did you arrive at this number?

_____

_____

_____

(1 being extremely unsatisfactory and ineffective and 10 being excellent and very effective)

(b) In what area(s) do you feel you're strongest as a parent? Where do you feel you need the most help?

_____

_____

_____

SENSEI SAYS...

"The best and only way to teach is by example. You cannot *not* teach—you are always teaching by your actions, attitudes, and behaviors. The way you talk, the way you walk, the way you breathe, the way you believe—that's what they are watching. So if you want your kids to get better, you have to get better."

—Mike Storms

(8) As parents, our actions speak louder than words. That is, when it comes to teaching our children to do the right thing, our *example* packs more punch than the things we say, which is especially true with our teenagers.

(a) What *positive* images do your kids mirror most from your life?

_____

_____

(b) What *negative* images do they mirror that you wish they wouldn't?

_____

_____

_____

(c) What can you do to change the negative images you see reflected?

_____

_____

_____

SENSEI SAYS...

"Your kids amplify what you do. In most cases, if you lie a little, your kids are going to lie a lot. If you drink a little, your kids are going to drink a lot. If you have a little temper, their temper will expand. About 25 percent of the way they behave is genetic; about 75 percent is the result of environment."

—Mike Storms

AGELESS ADVICE

"He who heeds instruction and correction is [not only himself] in the way of life [but also] *is a way of life* for others. And he who neglects or refuses reproof [not only himself] goes astray [but also] causes to err and is a path toward ruin for others."

—Proverbs 10:17 AMP

(9) Carefully *read* Proverbs 10:17 above. How do you think this applies to parenting your kids? Are there any adjustments in your life that you feel you need to make after reading this verse? If so, what are they?

_____

_____

_____

_____

_____

_____

(10) There is only one perfect parent and that is our *Heavenly Father*. He stands ready, willing, and able to help you be the best parent you can be. He will show you how to make the needed adjustments to produce the positive change your children need.

(a) *Read* **Psalm 25:9, 12; 32:8.** What do these verses say to you about receiving wisdom and direction from God?

_____

_____

_____

(b) *Write* out and commit to memory the powerful promise of **James 1:5.**

_____

_____

_____

A PAGE FROM THE PLAYBOOK

"As children hear their parents praying for wisdom and direction, they learn that parents can't fix everything. I believe God designed it this way. After all, if parents were perfect, children would never sense their need for God."

—**Paul Meier**[5]

(11) The greatest thing you can do as a parent to help your children is to connect them to a vibrant, *personal relationship* with God. The internal, transforming power of His Holy Spirit living inside of them is the most powerful force for shaping their lives.

(a) How would you describe *your* relationship with God? How about your children's relationship with Him?

_____

_____

_____

(b) Why is a relationship with God so important for you and your children? What practical things can you do to improve this area of your life and theirs?

_____

_____

_____

Check out Matthew 6:33; Proverbs 3:5-8.

AGELESS ADVICE

"Everything else is worthless when compared with the priceless gain of knowing Christ Jesus my Lord. I have put aside all else, counting it worth less than nothing, in order that I can have Christ, and become one with him...."

—**Philippians 3:8,9 TLB**

Time to Reflect

Have you made mistakes as a parent? All of us have. Thankfully, God does not condemn us. On the contrary, He promises to give us wisdom and strength to help shape our children to be the best they can be and fulfill their divine destiny.

Take a few moments to get quiet before the Lord. Ask Him to forgive you of anything you've done wrong and for grace (strength) and wisdom to properly parent your children.

Now, write down anything else God is revealing to you through this study.

_____

_____

_____

_____

_____

_____

_____

_____

_____

_____

_____

_____

_____

_____

_____

_____

_____

_____

_____

_____

_____

_____

_____

_____

_____

_____

_____

_____

_____

_____

_____

_____

_____

_____

_____

_____

_____

(1)Karen Santorum, *Everyday Graces—A Child's Book of Good Manners* (Wilmington, DE: ISI Books, 2005) p. xiv. (2)*Demolishing Strongholds*, Leader's Guide, written and compiled by Holly Varnum (Petersburg, KY, Answers in Genesis, 2007) p.30. (3)Dr. James Dobson, *Preparing for Adolescence* (Ventura, CA: Gospel Light, 2006) pp. 48-49. (4)Raymond McHenry, *McHenry's Quips, Quotes & Other Notes* (Peabody, MA: Hendrickson Publishers, Inc., 2004) pp. 53-54. (5)*365 Day Brighteners Celebrating Mothers* (Siloam Springs, AR: Garborg's®, A brand of Dayspring® Cards, Inc., 2005) February 3.

Chapter 2

Harnessing the Power of Your Words

"Words have an incredible power to build us up or tear us down emotionally. This is particularly true when it comes to giving or gaining family approval. Many people can clearly remember words of praise their parents spoke years ago. Others can remember negative words they heard—and what their parents were wearing when they spoke them! ...If you are a parent, your children desperately need to hear a spoken blessing from you."

—Gary Smalley & John Trent, Ph.D.[1]

Chapter 2

Harnessing the Power of Your Words

Please refer to Chapter 2 in the *Parenting 101* book along with Session 2 of the CD series.

SENSEI SAYS...

"Be careful what you say to your kids. Your **words**, more than anything else, will *define* them—even subtle ones. You can change the way your children are thinking and being imprinted by changing your words."

—Mike Storms

(1) Remember the old saying, "Sticks and stones can break my bones, but words can never hurt me"? Nothing could be further from the truth. Indeed, our words are powerful—so powerful that they produce the fruit of *life* or *death* in the hearer, especially our children.

    (a) *Write* out and commit to memory these powerful principles from Proverbs.

    PROVERBS 18:21

_____

_____

_____

    PROVERBS 13:3

_____

_____

_____

Also check out Proverbs 21:23.

(b) Two "fruits" of death often produced in our kids are fear and anger. What other forms of death can you think of? Are any of these operating in you or your children? If so, which ones?

_____

_____

_____

(c) Jesus is the Way, the Truth, and the **Life**. The more you are filled with His Spirit, the more life will be in your words. _Read_ Galatians 5:22,23 and jot down nine fruits of _life_ that your words can produce in your children.

_____

_____

_____

A PAGE FROM THE PLAYBOOK

"We often poison and wound each other, especially our children, with the words we use. You may have grown up with parents who used words as weapons, and you hoped you wouldn't do the same with your children. But you will probably repeat the pattern in some way—unless you become the transition person to break the pattern and develop healthy patterns of communication which reflect the presence of Jesus Christ. Such a change is possible!"
—**H. Norman Wright**[2]

AGELESS ADVICE

"Whoever of you loves life and desires to see many good days, *keep your tongue from evil* and your lips from speaking lies. Turn from evil and do good; seek peace and pursue it."
—**Psalm 34:12-14 NIV**

(2) The way we parent our kids has a lot to do with the way our parents raised us. From the methods we use to the words we speak, we often give out the same thing we received. This is especially true when the pressure is on and situations heat up.

(a) Looking back on your life, what are some of the phrases you remember hearing most from your parents? Can you remember the behavior that prompted these responses?

NEGATIVE PHRASES

_____

_____

_____

POSITIVE PHRASES

_____

_____

_____

(b) What phrases commonly come out of your mouth when correcting your kids? Do you see any connection with the words you heard as a child? If so, what is it?

NEGATIVE PHRASES

_____

_____

_____

POSITIVE PHRASES

_____

_____

_____

SENSEI SAYS...

"The behavior we're getting from our kids is a harvest of what we have *seeded* over and over again with our words. They believe what we say to them when they are young; they don't have a filter until they are eleven, twelve, or thirteen years old. So everything we say to them goes right into their *self-image* and is defined by us."

—Mike Storms

(3) Knowing that a parent's words greatly define their child's self-image, how did your parents' words help paint a picture of the way you see yourself? Describe it.

YOUR SELF-IMAGE

_____

_____

_____

What kind of "self" portrait do you think your children have of themselves as a result of your words? How would you like them to see themselves?

YOUR CHILDREN'S SELF-IMAGE

Child 1 _____

_____

_____

_____

Child 2 _____

_____

_____

_____

Child 3 _____

_____

_____

_____

For a real eye-opening view of the affects of your words, ask your children how your words have impacted them.

TRUE STORY:

"SAY WHAT YOU WANT TO SEE"

Recently, we were having a party at our house, and someone introduced their young daughter to my wife and me. The introduction went as they usually do. "This is Sophie," the lady said, "and she's very shy." It was almost as if she was apologizing for her daughter. Sophie didn't seem shy to us. I've seen shy kids. They often dive behind their parents' legs and cling to them for dear life. They usually won't shake your hand, make eye contact, or even look in your direction.

Interestingly, once Sophie's mom was out of sight, she began smiling, laughing, and playing just like all the other kids. When her mom came back around her, Sophie started acting shy all over again. She acted just the way her mother *said*; the way she was expected to behave is the way she behaved.

Our children become what we say they are. If we repeatedly say to them that they are stubborn, lazy, rebellious, slow in school, or have ADD or ADHD, then that is what they will become. Instead, we need to tell them the positive things we see them becoming—great readers, great leaders, great friends to others, and every other godly quality we can find in Scripture. In Sophie's case, instead of saying she is shy, her parents can learn to say in a positive way that she is cautious and likes to get to know people gradually. Wow, what a difference our words make!

AGELESS ADVICE

"The right word at the right time is like a custom-made piece of jewelry."
—**Proverbs 25:11 The Message**

A PAGE FROM THE PLAYBOOK

"Building a positive, healthy, Christ-centered self-image in their children is one of the primary tasks of all parents. Frankly, we have seldom, if ever, seen a kid involved in drug abuse, suicide, or other crisis who has a healthy self-image. ...We can help our children by building up their self-image rather than tearing it down. Children who grow up in an environment full of put-downs, negative nicknames, and criticism often become critical adults whose self-esteem is less than adequate."

—Stephen Arterburn & Jim Burns[3]

(4) Thankfully, God's Word has a lot to say about our words and the way we *should* and *should not* speak to each other—including our children.

   (a) *Read* Ephesians 4:31 and Colossians 4:6 and identify what your speech toward your kids should be *full of* and what it should be *free of*. What do these verses say to you?

   _____

   _____

   _____

   (b) Carefully *read* Proverbs 12:18 and 15:1-7 and answer these questions:

   What does your *soft answer* do when talking to your kids?

   _____

   What is your *tone of voice* and *facial expression* while correcting them?

   _____

   _____

These also determine how "soft" your answer is. Tension in your voice and on your face can make even soft answers seem harsh.

What happens when you speak *harsh, rash* words?

_____

How is having a *wise, gentle* tongue a blessing to your children?

_____

What do these verses say to you?

_____

_____

_____

AGELESS ADVICE

"When words are many, sin is not absent, but he who holds his tongue is wise."

—Proverbs 10:19 NIV

A PAGE FROM THE PLAYBOOK

"Learn early to treat your children with appropriate *respect*. Give them some elbow room once in a while until they're ready to talk. Don't tease them if they're bugged by something—especially the opposite sex. And don't ever blab secrets they've told you in confidence. That will come back to haunt you."

—Greg Johnson and Mike Yorkey[4]

(5) Teaching our children *respect* is very important. If they don't respect us as parents, they will probably not respect others in authority either, including God. Receiving

respect from our kids begins with *giving* them respect. What we sow, is what we will reap.

(a) How would you describe the way you speak to your children—respectfully or disrespectfully? How about your nonverbal communication?

_____

_____

_____

(b) Are you open to allowing your kids to *respectfully* tell you anything that is on their heart? If *yes*, how has it strengthened your relationship? If *no*, why?

_____

_____

_____

(6) Part of showing respect is learning how to be a good *listener*. God gave us two ears and one mouth. That means we probably ought to listen twice as much as we speak.

(a) In your own words, describe someone who is a good **listener**.

_____

_____

_____

(b) In light of your definition, are you a good listener to your kids? What needs to change in your life to make you a better listener?

_____

_____

_____

(c) *Write* out James 1:19 and hide it in your heart.

JAMES 1:19

_____

_____

_____

AGELESS ADVICE

"For everything there is a season, a time for every activity under heaven. ...A time to *be quiet* and a time to speak."
—**Ecclesiastes 3:1, 7 NLT**

(7) By now, you have a better understanding of the weight of your words. How can you change what is coming out of your mouth? The key is identifying and changing what is in your *heart*. Jesus said, "...Out of the abundance of the heart the mouth speaks" (Matthew 12:34 NKJV).

(a) What frustrates and irritates you most about your kids?

_____

_____

_____

(b) Is there something else that is frustrating you *more than* your kids, such as your job or your relationship with your spouse? If so, explain what it is.

_____

_____

_____

(c) God does not want you to live frustrated, irritated, and aggravated all the time. Take a moment to get quiet before Him and humbly ask Him to show you your heart—why you feel the way you feel. *Write* what He reveals and surrender it to Him in prayer.

_____

_____

_____

A PAGE FROM THE PLAYBOOK

"Frustration doesn't have to lead to an angry reaction. You are free to decide how you will respond to it. Problems, difficulties, disappointments, heartaches and failures are an unavoidable part of parenting. ...Your children will try your patience, irritate you and sometimes humiliate you in ways you never thought possible. But you can respond with words that heal instead of words that wound. It's *your* choice."

—H. Norman Wright[5]

(8) One of the most important aspects of harnessing the power of our words is keeping an open line of communication between us and our children. And mealtime is a great time to connect. Having at least one meal a day or five meals a week together as a family can work wonders!

(a) Describe the atmosphere around the dinner table when you were a kid. How does it compare with the meals you share with your family?

_____

_____

_____

(b) How many times a week do you sit down and eat a meal with your children? If it is less than five, what could you adjust in your schedule to increase it?

_____

_____

_____

(c) Are meals with your children something you *dread* or *enjoy*? Why? What can you change to make mealtime a more positive, energizing experience?

_____

_____

_____

SOMETHING TO THINK ABOUT

QUIP TIPS FOR MAKING THE MOST OF MEALTIME————

♦ Turn off the television

♦ Develop some kid-friendly, conversation-starting questions (ahead of time)

♦ Play instrumental or praise music quietly in the background

♦ Keep the conversation light—avoid dealing with major behavior issues

(9) To help you better connect with them, plan a special date with each of them. Take them on a picnic in the park or for lunch at a local restaurant. Ask them some simple questions like the ones below, and let the conversation flow!

FIND OUT THEIR FAVORITES!

What is your favorite...

Color _____ Game/Sport _____ Movie _____

Snack/Treat _____ Restaurant _____

Season of the Year _____ Holiday _____
Subjects in School _____
Type of Music _____ Song _____
Book of the Bible _____ Scripture _____

What are your top three, most enjoyable...

Meals We Eat _____
Outdoor Activities _____
Indoor Activities _____
Places You'd Like to Visit _____

OTHER ODDS AND ENDS

Who is your best friend? What is it about them that you like so much?

_____

What do you dream of being/doing when you grow up? Why?

_____

What is one of your greatest fears? (Then share one of your greatest fears with them.)

_____

Describe the kind of person you want to marry and share your life with.

_____

What things do you like most about our family? If there was one thing you could change, what would it be?

_____

Feel free to adjust or omit any of the questions to fit your child's level of maturity. If the conversation takes an unexpected turn, relax and go with the flow. You're connecting with your kids, and that's what it is all about!

A PAGE FROM THE PLAYBOOK

"...For all of us, our communication skills directly relate to how successful we'll be in our marriages, families, friendships, and professions. And if we're serious about having meaningful, fulfilling, productive relationships, we can't afford to let inadequate communication skills carry our conversations. There's got to be a better way of connecting with others in our lives—a way that can guide us safely into the depths of love."

—Gary Smalley and John Trent, Ph.D.[6]

(10) Carefully *read* Psalm 141:3 and Psalm 19:14. Now, take a moment and write a prayer for God's help that reflects your heart and the heart of these verses.

MY PRAYER

_____

_____

_____

_____

_____

AGELESS ADVICE

"Set a guard, O Lord, over my mouth; keep watch over the door of my lips."

—Psalm 141:3 NASB

"May the *words* of my mouth and the meditation of my heart be pleasing in your sight, O Lord, my Rock and my Redeemer."

—Psalm 19:14 NIV

Time to Reflect

SENSEI SAYS...

"When you do or say something wrong to your kids, go apologize. That is a big thing. Then they can see that when you are not perfect, you are going to admit it."

—Mike Storms

Take a few moments to stop and examine your heart. Have you been using words and phrases with your kids that you know have hurt them? Are they similar to the things you heard spoken to you while growing up? God is not mad at you. He loves you and wants to heal the hurt in your heart as well as the wounds in your children. Go to Him now and ask Him to forgive you and heal you. He will give you the ability to learn a new language—the language of love that brings correction in a constructive way. Write anything He speaks to your heart as you sit in His presence.

_____

_____

_____

_____

_____

_____

_____

_____

_____

(1) Gary Smalley and John Trent, Ph.D., *The Blessing* (New York, NY: Pocket Books, a division of Simon & Schuster, Inc., 1986) pp. 54-55. (2) H. Norman Wright, *The Power of a Parent's Words* (Ventura, CA: Regal Books, a division of GL Publications, 1991) p. 96. (3) Stephen Arterburn & Jim Burns, *Parents Guide to Top 10 Dangers Teens Face* (Wheaton, IL, A Focus on the Family Book published by Tyndale House Publishers, 1995) pp. 288-290. (4) Greg Johnson and Mike Yorkey, *Faithful Parents, Faithful Kids* (Wheaton, IL: Tyndale House Publishers, Inc., 1993) pp. 120-121. (5) See note 2, p. 120. (6) Gary Smalley and John Trent, Ph.D., *The Language of Love* (Pomona, CA: Focus on the Family Publishing, 1988) p. 8.

Chapter 3

Employing the Power of Praise

"Parents dishonor their children not only by harsh or negative words they speak, but also by neglecting to communicate *praise* or *acceptance* at the appropriate time. Children require frequent encouragement, direction, and affirmation. They need to be told, as well as shown, they are loved and valued. If not, chances are good they'll seek it in the wrong places."

—John Bevere[1]

Chapter 3

Employing the Power of Praise

Please refer to Chapter 3 in the *Parenting 101* book along with Session 3 of the CD series.

SENSEI SAYS...

"Words are powerful things. You are either in the construction or demolition business—you choose. Make sure your words are positive and that they are creating a bright future for your kids. Build big dreams for them. Yes, the world is a negative, nasty place, but it's also a beautiful place. It just depends on the lenses you are looking through."

—**Mike Storms**

(1) Words of praise are a powerful force to positively shape the lives of our children. In fact, one of the most effective ways to bring them correction is to "sandwich" it between words of praise. This is the PCP Principle—Praise, Correction, Praise.

    (a) *Read* Proverbs 3:27. How do you think this verse relates to praising your children?

    _____

    _____

    _____

    (b) According to Ephesians 4:29 and Romans 15:2, what should be the aim of your words toward your children?

    _____

    _____

    _____

(c) *Write* out Ephesians 4:29 and hide it in your heart. What does this verse say to you?

EPHESIANS 4:29

_____

_____

_____

AGELESS ADVICE

"Fathers, do not irritate and provoke your children to anger [do not exasperate them to resentment], but rear them [tenderly] in the training and discipline and the counsel and admonition of the Lord."

—Ephesians 6:4 AMP

(2) As strange as it may seem, children do not understand and process negative commands in the way they are intended. When we say, "Stop acting like a fool," their mind hears, "I am a fool." With this in mind, take the following negative statements and *rewrite* them in a positive way.

NEGATIVE, DESTRUCTIVE STATEMENT	POSITIVE, CONSTRUCTIVE ALTERNATIVE
"Boy, you are hard-headed."	_____
"You are as sneaky as a snake."	_____
"Can't you do anything right?"	_____
"You're so picky."	_____
"You are such a pain."	_____
"How many times do I have to tell you?"	_____
"When are you going to learn to keep your mouth shut?"	_____
"I just don't know what I'm going to do with you."	_____

A PAGE FROM THE PLAYBOOK

"...The opposite of criticism is one of the most powerful motivating forces available to parents—*praise*. It can be used in a variety of ways. You might give your children ribbons for good behavior. You could take a picture of your child doing something that you really appreciate and put it in an album or hang it on the wall for everyone to see. ...As parents, we can motivate our children through praise. Instead of mentioning to them the two things they did wrong today, let's talk to them about the ten things they did right. You'll be amazed at the results."

—**Gary Smalley**[2]

(3) Studies show that the average amount of time a father spends talking to his children each day is sixty seconds or less, and most of that time is spent pointing out negative behavior.[3] With this in mind, if you had only a minute to talk to and pour into your children each day, what would you say?

_____

_____

_____

(4) Clearly, it is much easier to praise our children if we feel they are *successful*. This is especially true for our kids as they grow older. With this in mind, what would your son and/or daughter have to do (at their age and place in life) for you to consider them a success?

MY DEFINITION OF SUCCESS FOR _____ IS...

_____

_____

_____

Carefully *read* what you have written. Which part(s) of your definition of success lines up with God's Word? Does any part *not* line up with Scripture and need to be tweaked? If so, what part?

_____

_____

_____

A PAGE FROM THE PLAYBOOK

"All of our communication with our children, including constructive guidance, should be *nurturing*. Nurturing communication fosters a loving, trusting parent-child relationship. Nurturing words build, support, encourage and express caring. The child with fault-finding parents becomes the prisoner of his own negative feelings. But the child who grows up in an atmosphere of encouragement is released to develop emotionally and is open to experiencing God's grace."

—H. Norman Wright[4]

(5) Few things make us feel better than knowing our parents love us unconditionally and are proud of us. It puts a spring in our step and confidence in our heart.

(a) Do you know that your parents *love* you? Do you know that they are *proud* of you? If so, how—what have they done or said over the years to show it?

_____

_____

_____

If your parents have not expressed love to you, it may be that they didn't receive it themselves. Know that God loves you intensely and yearns to be welcome in your life! (See Ephesians 2:4,5; 1 John 3:1; 4:9,10.)

(b) Ask each of your children to honestly answer these same two questions and write their responses.

CHILD 1: _____

"The top three ways that I know Mom and Dad *love* me are..."

1)_____

2)_____

3)_____

"The top three ways that I know Mom and Dad are *proud* of me are..."

1)_____

2)_____

3)_____

CHILD 2: _____

"The top three ways that I know Mom and Dad *love* me are..."

1)_____

2)_____

3)_____

"The top three ways that I know Mom and Dad are *proud* of me are..."

1)_____

2)_____

3)_____

CHILD 3: _____

"The top three ways that I know Mom and Dad *love* me are..."

1)_____

2)_____

3)_____

"The top three ways that I know Mom and Dad are *proud* of me are..."

1)_____

2)_____

3)_____

(c) What eye-opening information did you learn from their answers? What changes do you feel you need to make as a result? _____

_____

_____

_____

Note: God's love for us is unconditional, and our love for our children should be unconditional too. If your children gave answers that are primarily performance or behavior based and not character based, your love and appreciation is more conditional. Ask God to bring balance to this area of your life.

SENSEI SAYS...

"Seed the behavior you want. Don't keep seeding and watering the behavior you don't want with words like, 'You never listen,' 'What's wrong with you?' and 'You'll never change.' Your kids' wrong behavior will not change if it is being reinforced by your words."

—Mike Storms

(6) More than likely, you are dealing with a situation with one (or more) of your children in which you have repeatedly tried to get them to change their poor behavior, but it has not worked.

(a) Briefly describe the situation, including what you have done/said.

_____

_____

_____

(b) Using the PCP Principle—Praise, Correction, Praise—
write a more positive approach you can take

_____

_____

_____

SOMETHING TO THINK ABOUT

A PROVEN RECIPE FOR REWARDING WITH PRAISE

♦ Always be sincere.

♦ Always be specific.

♦ Praise your child's efforts more than his abilities.

♦ Use praise to encourage and motivate, not manipulate.

♦ Focus on your child's individual achievements; avoid comparing your kids.

♦ Smile, make eye contact, and give them a hug.

A PAGE FROM THE PLAYBOOK

"Spare the rod and spoil the child—that is true. But, beside the rod, keep an apple to give him when he has done well."

—**Martin Luther**[5]

(7) Pre-framing behavior is a very effective method of producing positive change in your children. *Read* each of the pretend scenarios and come up with a positive way you can pre-frame the behavior change you want to see.

PRE-FRAME – *TAKE ONE*

You're taking your kids to a restaurant and you want them to be polite, not fight, and enjoy the night. How will you pre-frame their behavior ahead of time?

_____

_____

_____

PRE-FRAME – *TAKE TWO*

It's time for the weekly grocery trip; you want your kids to not climb the shelves, throw stuff in the basket, or ask for everything they see and whine when they can't have it. How will you pre-frame their behavior ahead of time?

_____

_____

_____

PRE-FRAME – *TAKE THREE*

It's Saturday and tomorrow is church. You want your kids to get their baths tonight, pick out their clothes, and get up early enough to get dressed, have breakfast, and arrive at church on time—without fighting. How will you pre-frame their behavior?

_____

_____

_____

SENSEI SAYS...

"**Pre-frame** the behavior you *want* and *expect* from your children. Tell them ahead of time in a positive and affirming way how you want them to act. Then tell that you know they can do it. Pour into them statements like, 'I know you can do this. Show me how good you can be. Make me proud!'"

—**Mike Storms**

(8) As parents, there are periods in our life when all we can see is our child's flaws and failures. It is as if a huge magnifying glass has been placed before them, glaringly revealing every error they make. Have you been there, done that, and bought the T-shirt?

(a) Carefully *read* Revelation 12:9,10, 1 Peter 5:8, and John 10:10. In light of these verses, who's behind the fault-finding thoughts you are hearing? What is his purpose?

_____

_____

_____

(b) To combat this invasion of accusation, you are going to have to *purposely* think good thoughts about your child. Meditate on the message of Philippians 4:8; then make a list of every positive quality he or she has, and begin to *fix your mind* on them.

I WILL FIX MY MIND ON THESE POSITIVE QUALITIES IN

_____:

_____

_____

_____

_____

(9) In order to more fully apply the principle of Philippians 4:8, we need to learn to be "good finders." In other words, in addition to correcting our children's wrong behavior, we are also to focus on finding the good things they are doing and praise them for it.

(a) *Read* Proverbs 11:27 and identify the blessing of being a good finder and the consequences of only looking for what's wrong.

_____

_____

_____

(b) In what practical ways do you think you can implement this tool in your parenting?

_____

_____

_____

(c) How can you teach your children to be good finders, and in what ways will this benefit them as a person?

_____

_____

_____

SOMETHING TO THINK ABOUT

A survey asked mothers to keep track of how many times they made negative, compared with positive, comments to their children. They admitted that they criticized *ten* times for every time they said something favorable. A three-year survey in one city's schools found that the teachers were 75% negative. The study indicated that it takes *four* positive statements from a teacher to offset the effects of one negative statement to a child.

—Institute of Family Relations[6]

A PAGE FROM THE PLAYBOOK

"...Each child is gifted in some particular area. Your goal as a parent is to recognize that area of strength and emphasize it as your child develops, for in these areas of strength lies your child's greatest potential for excellence. By cultivating these areas, you will do great things for your child's self-esteem as well."

—Charles Stanley[7]

(10) Romans 12:6 NIV says, "We have different gifts, according to the grace given us...." This includes our children. By helping them discover their God-given gifts and who He made them to be, you show them that you believe in them and, consequently, build their confidence and self-esteem.

BECOME YOUR CHILD'S TALENT SCOUT

What activities or sports are your children naturally gifted in that they also enjoy?

_____

_____

_____

Have you been encouraging and praising them in their gift(s)? If so, how?

_____

_____

_____

Is there anything else you can do to help them develop their gift(s) more? What is it?

_____

_____

_____

If you don't know what your child's gifts are, pray and ask God to show you. Once He does, become their greatest cheerleader. Be careful not to withhold encouragement and praise from them because you have no interest in the area of their talent.

AGELESS ADVICE

"Train up a child in the way he should go [and *in keeping with his individual gift or bent*], and when he is old he will not depart from it."

—Proverbs 22:6 AMP

(11) The greatest thing you can speak over and into your children are the powerful promises of God's Word. Think for a moment. What godly character qualities would you like to see God develop in the lives of your children? *Write* them down along with any specific scripture references that support them (using a Bible concordance will be helpful).

THE CHARACTER QUALITIES I WANT TO SEE GOD DEVELOP IN MY CHILDREN ARE...

_____

_____

_____

Begin to pray for these traits to become a reality. Speak them over your children, calling those things that be not as though they are, just as God does (see Romans 4:17). Remember, the creative power of life is in your tongue. Use it to positively shape your kids!

TRUE STORY:

"A WHALE OF A TALE"

How do the people at Sea World find killer whales that can jump twenty feet in the air? Do they charter a huge seafaring ship, look for whales that are jumping twenty feet out of the water, and catch them? No. They catch a whale and then *train* it to jump. They start by putting a pole in the water and encouraging the whale to swim over it. When he does, he is rewarded with a bucket of fish. The trainers then move the pole up higher and encourage the whale to swim over it again. When he does, another bucket of fish is given to him as a reward. Again and again, the trainers raise the bar higher and higher, rewarding the whale with fish every time he successfully makes the jump.

In the same way, we need to **reward approximations of success**. The first time my kids cut the lawn, it looked like someone chewed it up and spit it out. But I kept coaching them on how to do it. I told them, "Okay guys. After three runs, empty the grass catcher. Make sure to fill the machine with gas before you start so that you don't run out and have to fill it up in the middle of the job. And cut it in alternating patterns so that it looks good." With each level of improvement, or approximation of success, I rewarded them. This method has made a positive impact on my kids, and it will do the same for yours too.

Time to Reflect

SENSEI SAYS...

"Learn the language of praise and approval. Don't just be fluent in the language of criticism and disapproval. Be a *good finder*. Make sure you are praising your kids three times as much as you are correcting them. When he or she achieves the behavior you have been trying to teach them, throw them a 'praise party.'"

—Mike Storms

As you come to the end of this lesson, take some time to reflect upon the things God is showing you—in His Word and in your life. What scriptures really stood out that you want to commit to memory? What principles helped you see a side of things you have never seen before? Get quiet before God and ask Him for wisdom and strength to put the power of praise into practice in your home.

_____

_____

_____

_____

_____

_____

_____

_____

_____

_____

———————————————————————

———————————————————————

———————————————————————

———————————————————————

———————————————————————

———————————————————————

———————————————————————

———————————————————————

———————————————————————

———————————————————————

———————————————————————

———————————————————————

(1) John Bevere, *Honor's Reward* (New York, NY: FaithWords, Hachette Book Group, 2007) p. 178. (2) Gary Smalley, *The Key to Your Child's Heart* (Dallas, TX: Word Publishing, 1992) pp. 167-168. (3) Ibid, p. 167. (4) H. Norman Wright, *The Power of a Parent's Words* (Ventura, CA: Regal Books, a division of GL Publications, 1991) p. 108. (5) Quotes on *Children & Family* (http://dailychristianquote.com/dcqfamily.html, retrieved 4/29/10). (6) Illustrations on *Criticism* (http://bible.org/ illustration/ten-one, retrieved 4/28/10). (7) Charles Stanley, *How to Keep Your Kids on Your Team* (Nashville, TN, Oliver-Nelson Books, a division of Thomas Nelson, Inc. Publishers, 1986) p. 53.

Chapter 4

Creating Change Through Consequences and Consistency

"Discipline is a training process. The primary purpose of parental discipline is to teach responsibility rather than to evoke obedience. This means consistently helping our children understand that most of life involves choices and consequences. Discipline in the home should consist of setting clearly defined limits with our children. ...As kids understand that their actions have consequences, they learn to live life properly."

—Stephen Arterburn & Jim Burns[1]

Chapter 4

Creating Change Through Consequences and Consistency

Please refer to Chapter 4 in the *Parenting 101* book along with Session 4 of the CD series.

SENSEI SAYS...

"We don't have a crime problem in the U.S.—we have a *punishment problem.* People plea-bargain their way out of their punishment; they don't go to jail or they get out in a matter of months. In the same way, you don't have a behavior problem in your house—you have a follow-through or enforcement problem. Inconsistent discipline and enforcement of consequences leads to rebellion."

—Mike Storms

(1) It's been said that the indispensable link between desire and destiny is *discipline.* Your kids are destined by God to do great things—the desire has actually been planted deep within their heart. But in order for their destiny to become a reality, you must bring discipline to their lives.

(a) Briefly describe the kind of discipline, consequences, and punishments you received from your parents.

_____

_____

_____

(b) What things did they do to effectively teach and correct you—what worked?

_____

_____

(c) What did they do that you intensely disliked and don't want to repeat with your kids?

_____

_____

PRESS PAUSE Does the memory of these things stir up anger and rage toward your parents? It may be that you are unknowingly holding on to unforgiveness. Take a moment to pray. As an act of your will, release your parents into God's hands; ask Him to forgive you of holding on to any unforgiveness and to heal the wounds in your soul. Lastly, pray for God to bless them. This will bring new freedom to your life and help keep you from repeating the same pattern of behavior with your kids.

SOMETHING TO THINK ABOUT

Discipline means "to instruct or educate; to inform the mind; to prepare by instructing in correct principles and habits; to teach rules and practice; to correct, chastise, or punish."[2] The words *punish* and *chastise* are very closely related and carry with them the meaning of inflicting physical pain, such as a spanking, to purify the motives of the heart and redirect the person back on the path of right.

(2) The best time to deal with improper behavior is *when it starts*. The moment you recognize wrong attitudes and actions developing, prune them—nip them in the bud.

(a) In what areas do you feel your children need to change the most—where do they need the most discipline?

_____

_____

_____

(b) Is there any connection between these areas and things in your own life where you need discipline? If so, what is it?

_____

_____

_____

(c) In order to experience any lasting, positive change, there is a crucial component that must be included in the equation. *Read* John 15:5 and tell what that is. Are you including this?

_____

_____

_____

Pray and invite God into your situation (and everything else too). Ask Him to show you a creative plan of correction in each of these areas through His Word, His people, and godly resources.

A Page from the Playbook

"Don't waste your time on threats. I haven't found that exact wording in my Bible, but I think the spirit of it—'Say what you mean, and do what you say'—is there. Threats will only teach kids the art of gambling. They ask themselves, *Will Mom really follow through this time?* Children know when the odds are in their favor, when it's worth the risk to push the limits. So don't say you're going to do anything you can't carry out. If you've established boundaries ahead of time and consequences for crossing them, be prepared to follow through."

—Lisa Whelchel[3]

(3) By definition, the word *consistent* means to be "fixed, firm, not fluid; uniform and not contradictory."[4] So being consistent in disciplining your kids means your standard of right

and wrong does not change; the rewards and consequences remain the same, and your kids know what to expect.

(a) If being *consistent* in your discipline creates credibility and credibility creates compliance or obedience, what do you think *inconsistency* creates in your children?

_____

_____

_____

(b) Are you consistent in your discipline? If not, what keeps you from being consistent?

_____

_____

_____

(c) If you are consistent, what benefits is it producing in your children and your relationship with them?

_____

_____

_____

AGELESS ADVICE

"For the time being no discipline brings joy, but seems grievous and painful; but afterwards it yields a *peaceable fruit of righteousness* to those who have been trained by it [a harvest of fruit which consists in righteousness—in conformity to God's will in purpose, thought, and action, resulting in right living and right standing with God]."
—**Hebrews 12:11 AMP**

(4) It's very important to keep reminding our kids of the behavior we want and not expect them to remember everything we told them. One of the greatest ways to do this is

by *posting the house rules* in one or more prominent, high-traffic areas, such as in the living room and near the kitchen table. Prayerfully and carefully make a list of the top ten rules (behaviors) you want your kids to learn. When possible, include a scripture to back it up.

Example: *Obey* and *Respect* Mom and Dad with your words, actions and attitudes.

Ephesians 6:1-3 – "Children, obey your parents in the Lord [as His representatives], for this is just and right. Honor (esteem and value as precious) your father and your mother—this is the first commandment with a promise—that all may be well with you and that you may live long on the earth."

THE TOP TEN RULES OF OUR HOUSE

1)_____

2)_____

3)_____

4)_____

5)_____

6)_____

7)_____

8)_____

9)_____

10)_____

Remember to review these rules on a regular basis to keep them fresh in your children's mind. Make it fun by turning it into a game. Offer a small reward like a sticker for each child who can recite from memory five or more. When all your kids can recite all ten, take them out for pizza!

(5) Now make a list of the top ten privileges your children enjoy—ten being the smallest and one being the biggest and most valuable.

THE TOP TEN PRIVILEGES MY KIDS ENJOY

1)_____

2)_____

3)_____

4)_____

5)_____

6)_____

7)_____

8)_____

9)_____

10)_____

Note: To get the most mileage out of this activity, develop a top ten list of privileges for each of your children. Having this information will help you match the most effective consequence to the wrong behavior.

A PAGE FROM THE PLAYBOOK

"...The overall objective during preadolescence is teaching the child that *actions have inevitable consequences.* One of the most serious casualties in a permissive society is the failure to connect those two factors: behavior and consequences. ...How does one connect behavior with consequences? By being willing to let the child experience a reasonable amount of pain or inconvenience when he behaves irresponsibly. ...The best approach is to expect boys and girls to carry the responsibility that is appropriate for their age and occasionally to taste the bitter fruit that irresponsibility bears."

—Dr. James Dobson[5]

(6) Each of our children's negative *actions* (unacceptable behaviors) requires a specific *consequence.* And when we can connect the consequence to the behavior we are trying

to change, we will get better, faster results. Once we have given them a warning (no more than two) for wrong behavior, consequences must be carried out. *Read* through the list of unacceptable behaviors and write a creative consequence for each in the space provided.

UNACCEPTABLE BEHAVIOR	CREATIVE CONSEQUENCE TO BRING CHANGE
Neglecting to, or won't, clean up room; not completing, or won't, do chores.	_____
Leaving messes around the house	_____
Running or throwing things in the house.	_____
Hitting, kicking, or spitting on siblings or peers.	_____
Being unkind to siblings or others.	_____
Whining and complaining.	_____
Throwing a temper tantrum/fit.	_____
Refusing to eat or complaining about food.	_____
Being disrespectful to parents or others in authority.	_____
Telling lies.	_____
Stealing something from the store or another person.	_____
Not completing homework.	_____
Breaking curfew.	_____

In each situation, make sure that the punishment fits the crime—take away a privilege from them that best fits with what they did wrong. To help you with this, look back at question 5 as well as question 1 in chapter 1 and refresh yourself on the privileges your children enjoy. Keep in mind, the goal is for your children to become responsible and build self-control.

SENSEI SAYS...

"Consequences for wrong behavior must be clearly communicated and consistently enforced. Consistency creates credibility; credibility creates compliance (obedience)."

—Mike Storms

(7) Once we have decided in advance (DIA) on an appropriate consequence for our children's wrong behavior, we have to learn how to correct them with the right attitude.

(a) Why is disciplining in anger and yelling one of the worst ways to give correction?

_____

_____

_____

Check out Proverbs 14:17; Ecclesiastes 7:9.

(b) What is the best way to serve your children their consequences? Why?

_____

_____

_____

(c) Carefully *read* James 1:19,20. What are these verses, especially verse 20, speaking to you?

_____

_____

_____

AGELESS ADVICE

"Understand [this], my beloved brethren. Let every man be quick to hear [a ready listener], slow to speak, slow to take offense and to get angry. For man's anger does not promote the righteousness God [wishes and requires]."

—James 1:19,20 AMP

SENSEI SAYS...

"Don't embitter your kids. Temper everything you do with wisdom and love, not emotions (feelings). Don't let your emotions take the lead in your discipline. Give them discipline, but give it in a calm, cool, and considerate manner."

—Mike Storms

(8) Two other important things to remember regarding discipline for unacceptable behavior is to deal with your children quickly and punish them "until further notice" instead of a set time frame.

(a) Why is it important to give out *swift*, appropriate consequences? How does this affect your other children?

_____

_____

_____

(b) How is an open-ended punishment valuable and how does it help your kids become good decision makers?_____

_____

_____

_____

(c) Why is it vital for moms and dads to be in *unity* on issues of discipline? What are the benefits?

_____

_____

_____

Check out Matthew 12:25; 2 Corinthians 13:11; Psalm 133.

AGELESS ADVICE

"When the sentence for a crime is not quickly carried out, the hearts of the people are filled with schemes to do wrong."
—Ecclesiastes 8:11 NIV

A PAGE FROM THE PLAYBOOK

"To *chastise* means 'to inflict punishment or suffering upon, with a view to amendment; also simply, to punish, to inflict punishment (esp. corporal punishment) on.' When this definition is related to child training, it means to use a rod to inflict pain sufficient to cause a child to correct his rebellion—or in other words, to restrain a child from *willful disobedience*. When your child has willfully broken the standards you have set for him, he must be corrected by chastisement."

—J. Richard Fugate[6]

(9) If there was ever a parenting topic that stirred up a cloud of controversy, the use of corporal punishment, or spanking, would probably be at the top of the list. Many people have opinions on the topic, but what does God have to say? Carefully *read* through these scriptures and answer the questions that follow.

"He who spares his rod [of discipline] hates his son, but he who loves him disciplines diligently and punishes him early."

—Proverbs 13:24 AMP

"Discipline your children while there is hope. Otherwise you will ruin their lives."

—Proverbs 19:18 NLT

"Foolishness is bound up in the heart of a child; the rod of discipline will remove it far from him."

—Proverbs 22:15 NASB

"Don't be afraid to correct your young ones; a spanking won't kill them. A good spanking, in fact, might save them from something worse than death [*meaning Hell*]."

—Proverbs 23:13,14 The Message

"The rod of correction imparts wisdom, but a child left to himself disgraces his mother."

—Proverbs 29:15 NIV

After meditating on these Bible verses, what is God showing you about spanking?

_____

_____

_____

What is the best time to begin administering spanking in your children's life?

_____

_____

_____

What does physical discipline demonstrate and communicate to your children?

_____

_____

_____

What are some of the *positive* results of disciplining with the rod?

_____

_____

_____

What are some *negative* consequences you can expect if you withhold the rod?

_____

_____

_____

SOMETHING TO THINK ABOUT

SUGGESTIONS ON SPANKING

- **WHY should we chasten/spank our kids?** Because God said to.

- **WHEN should we spank our kids?** Children ages 2 to 12 (approximately) should be spanked for *willful disobedience* and *dishonoring parents*.

- **WHAT should be used to give the spanking?** An appropriate-sized rod, ruler, or wooden spoon is recommended. Do not use your hands, as they are connected with comfort, care, love, and protection in the child's eyes.

♦ **WHERE should the spanking be administered?**
It should be confined to the buttocks area, which is
cushioned enough to allow the only permanent
memory to be in the mind.

♦ **HOW is spanking different than child abuse?**
Spanking must *never* be done in anger or when the
parent is out of control or when accompanied by
yelling and name calling. It should always be done *in
love* and *under control* for the vital goal of breaking
rebellion and developing submission to authority—
ultimately God's authority.

Again, these are *suggestions* based on biblical standards, common
sense, and reliable research from godly men and women. Pray and
ask the Lord to show you the best way to administer corporal punishment to each of your children. He knows what's best.

SENSEI SAYS...

"It's your responsibility as a parent to teach your children. If
you don't teach them, the teachers will. If the teachers don't
teach them, the principal will. If the principal doesn't teach
them, the school board will. If the school board doesn't teach
them, the police will. If the police don't teach them, the judge
will. If the judge doesn't teach them, the penitentiary will. If
the penitentiary doesn't teach them, the grave will. So you
are first in line and have the responsibility of teaching your
kids."

—**Mike Storms**

(10) So here are three "Big Questions" you need to answer in
order to effectively implement the principles in this

chapter. You'll do best to gather your kids together and ask for their input.

(a) Do your children know the *rules*?

_____

_____

_____

(b) Do your children know the specific *consequences* for breaking these rules?

_____

_____

_____

(c) If they don't know the rules or they don't know the consequences for breaking them, what practical things can you do to make sure they know them?

_____

_____

_____

A PAGE FROM THE PLAYBOOK

"Concerning discipline, you need to remember the three C's. Be *clear* in communicating what you intend to do. Be *consistent* in your implementation. Be sure your disciplinary action *corresponds* to the transgression. ...Discipline will be effective only if the consequences of disobedience are in proportion to what the children did. If the consequences are too strict, children may rebel even more."

—**Charles Stanley**[7]

True Story:

"LET 'EM FEEL THE PAIN"

Over the years, I have had the good fortune of having dozens of grandparents bring their grandchildren to our karate school. After they had been with us for awhile and I established a good relationship with them, I asked them, "Why are you bringing your grandkids to karate? Where are their parents?" In most cases, I would hear that their parents were in prison, they had skipped town, or they were dead from a drug overdose.

In light of their answers, I then respectfully asked them, "If you could turn back the clock and go back to when they were kids, what would you do differently—what would you change?" Amazingly, almost every grandparent answered, "I didn't let them feel the consequences of their actions; I made excuses for them, I cut them slack, and I wish I hadn't. I knew the teacher, the principal, the judge, the cop, and I got them out of trouble. So they never learned the consequences of wrong choices when their troubles were a tiny sapling, and as a result their troubles grew into great oak trees."

As parents, you can learn a valuable lesson from the pain of others. Train your children when they are little. Let them feel the consequences of their inappropriate behavior. Consequences should be *smart*, *swift*, and *real*. If they are not listening to you and being polite when they are five, the situation will only become exponentially worse when they are seventeen. Remember, "Poverty and shame come to him who refuses instruction and correction, but he who heeds reproof is honored" (Proverbs 13:18 AMP).

Time to Reflect

SENSEI SAYS...

"You have two choices as a parent: You can *train the child* through discipline or *repair the adult* after he is grown. Discipline weighs ounces; regrets weigh tons. Train your children while they are little."

—Mike Storms

As you come to the conclusion of this lesson, pray and ask God to help you develop a specific plan of action for each of your children. He knows the perfect consequences that are needed in each situation that will bring about lasting change in your children's attitude, behavior, and character. While you are praying, also ask Him for the ability to remember the plan and be consistent in carrying it out. Consistency is the key to victory!

Take a few moments and write out a brief prayer to God. Invite Him into your home life afresh. Then jot down any other insights He sparks in your spirit. One idea from the Lord implemented in your home can change its course forever!

_____

_____

_____

_____

_____

_____

_____

_____

_____

_____

_____

_____

_____

_____

_____

_____

_____

_____

_____

_____

_____

_____

_____

_____

(1) Stephen Arterburn & Jim Burns, *Parents Guide to Top 10 Dangers Teens Face* (Wheaton, IL, A Focus on the Family Book published by Tyndale House Publishers, 1995) pp. 278-279. (2) Adapted from Noah Webster's *American Dictionary of the English Language, 1828* (San Francisco, CA: Foundation for American Christian Education, 1995). (3) Lisa Whelchel, *Creative Correction* (Wheaton, IL: Tyndale House Publishers, Inc., 2005) pp.136-137. (4) See note 2. (5) James C. Dobson, *The New Dare to Discipline* (Wheaton, IL: Tyndale House Publishers, Inc., 1992) pp. 115-117. (6) J. Richard Fugate, *What the Bible Says About Child Training* (Apache Junction, AZ: Foundation for Biblical Research, 1996) p. 167. (7) Charles Stanley, *How to Keep Your Kids on Your Team* (Nashville, TN, Oliver-Nelson Books, a division of Thomas Nelson, Inc. Publishers, 1986) pp. 82-83.

Chapter 5

Motivating Your Kids in Key Areas

"The first educational psychologist, E. L. Thorndike, developed an understanding of behavior in the 1920s that can be very useful for parents. He called it the '**law of reinforcement**.' ...Stated simply, the law of reinforcement reads, 'Behavior which achieves desirable consequences will recur.' In other words, if an individual likes what happens as a result of his behavior, he will be inclined to repeat that act."

—Dr. James Dobson[1]

Chapter 5

Motivating Your Kids in Key Areas

Please refer to Chapter 5 in the *Parenting 101* book along with Session 5 of the CD series.

SENSEI SAYS...

"Teach your kids when they are in a positive, upbeat emotional and mental state. This would include times such as relaxing at the beach, coming home from a restaurant or movie, or driving in the car to a vacation destination. Times like these allow your words of wisdom and instruction to penetrate deeply into their hearts and minds. Never try to teach them when they are angry or sad."

—**Mike Storms**

(1) Raising and teaching children in a good environment is essential to motivating them to make positive, healthy choices. Environment not only includes the atmosphere of our home but also the atmosphere, or quality, of our relationships with them.

(a) Generally speaking, how would you describe the overall atmosphere of your home? *Circle all the words that apply.*

peaceful chaotic quiet laughter-filled strife-filled
cold warm loving welcoming serious lighthearted
caring boring friendly depressing free controlling
safe dark cheerful refreshing encouraging negative

(b) As a whole, how would you describe your relationships with your children? *Circle all the words that apply.*

dear closed excellent understanding connected
distant open close strained affectionate one-way
indifferent trusting ordinary dull energizing
in conflict inspiring gloomy happy secure
vulnerable destructive positive

(c) Look back at the words you circled. Do you see a pattern? What does this say to you? How would you like the atmosphere of your home and relationships to change?

_____

_____

_____

For some eye-opening feedback, photocopy questions a and b and ask your children to answer them.

A PAGE FROM THE PLAYBOOK

"Rules without relationship lead to rebellion."
—Josh McDowell[2]

AGELESS ADVICE

"Don't you see that children are God's best gift? The fruit of the womb his generous legacy? Like a warrior's fistful of arrows are the children of a vigorous youth. Oh, how blessed are you parents, with your quivers full of children! Your enemies don't stand a chance against you; you'll sweep them right off your doorstep."
—Psalm 127:3-5 The Message

(2) Okay, so how close are you with your kids? This is another major factor when it comes to motivating them. The more connected you are in your *relationship*, the more you will be able to influence and motivate them to make right choices.

   (a) On average, how much time do you spend with your kids daily, focused on them or involved in an activity or task? How about weekly? Do you feel it is enough? If not, how can you increase it?

      _____

      _____

      _____

   (b) When was the last *meaningful* conversation you had with each of your children? Can you remember the topic and outcome of the discussion? If so, what was it?

      _____

      _____

      _____

   (c) When you look at your kids, how do you see them—as "half" a person or as growing people who are gifts from God? How is seeing them as valuable important to the quality of your relationships?

      _____

      _____

      _____

A PAGE FROM THE PLAYBOOK

"Someday your children are going to be making what you would consider 'big' decisions: where to go to college, who to room with, what to major in, whether or not to go to graduate school, which job to take, who to marry, and on and on. *Your influence then will be determined to a great degree by your involvement now.* You are in the process of setting a precedent with your children. You are either building credibility or destroying their confidence in you as an interested party. Again, your influence and involvement in helping your children make life's major decisions will be determined by your involvement now in life's mundane decisions. You must earn your right to be heard."

—**Charles Stanley**[3]

(3) One of the greatest things we can teach our children is the importance and power of an *attitude of gratitude.* Indeed, gratitude is the mother of all virtues—it is the fertile soil of the soul from which all other good things grow. Children who are truly thankful are more positive, peaceful, and easily motivated to do what's right than those who are ungrateful.

(a) Having an attitude of gratitude and being at peace are closely connected. According to Isaiah 26:3, how do we gain and maintain peace? What would make us lose peace?

_____

_____

_____

(b) *Write* out and commit to memory these words of wisdom regarding thankfulness.

1 THESSALONIANS 5:16-18

_____

_____

_____

PSALM 100:4

_____

_____

_____

A PAGE FROM THE PLAYBOOK

"...Having good manners, including expressing gratitude, is a great asset. When we neglect to require our children to say 'thank you' when somebody gives them a gift, says something nice about them, or does something for them, we are raising ungrateful children who are highly unlikely to be happy. Without gratitude, happiness is a rare thing. _With_ gratitude, the odds go up dramatically that happiness will be the result."

—**Zig Ziglar**[4]

(4) Is your attitude or your kids' attitudes taking a nosedive into negativity? Stop and count your blessings! On purpose, _take a trip down memory lane_ with your kids and begin to remember the ways God has blessed you and the things He has brought you through. Jot down the top ten memories that mean the most and begin to meditate on them.

The Top Ten Greatest Things I Am Thankful For Are...

1)_____

2)_____

3)_____

4)_____

5)_____

6)_____

7)_____

8)_____

9)_____

10)_____

My Child's Top Ten Greatest Things He/She Is Thankful For Are...

1)_____

2)_____

3)_____

4)_____

5)_____

6)_____

7)_____

8)_____

9)_____

10)_____

This life-giving activity can be repeated anytime, anywhere, whenever your attitude needs adjusting. An attitude of gratitude—what a wonderful habit to help your children develop!

SOMETHING TO THINK ABOUT

Motivating Kids in the Kitchen

How can you motivate kids to eat healthy? Here are some helpful tips:

♦ **Begin when they're young** – Introduce vegetables first, followed by fruit.

♦ **Serve fun finger foods** – Include things like baby carrots, celery stalks, broccoli florets, grapes, apple slices, and almonds as soon as they are able to safely chew and swallow.

♦ **Dish out healthy desserts** – Offer low-fat yogurt with honey, strawberries with real whipped cream, or baked bananas sprinkled with cinnamon and crushed pecans.

♦ **Take 'em shopping** - Allow them to see, smell, and feel an assortment of fresh veggies and fruit and choose some of the ones they want to try.

♦ **Educate them** – As they get older, show them how food companies market unhealthy foods to children.

♦ **Be an example** – Research shows that kids' eating habits are greatly influenced by what parents eat.

(5) Is sibling rivalry a problem? You're not alone. Fighting in the family goes way back. Teaching your children the timeless truths of God's Word found in the scriptures listed below will certainly help promote peace. *Write* out these scriptures and teach them to your children. Not only will you be amazed that they can recite the verses but also how Scripture changes their behavior.

PURSUE PEACE – PSALM 133:1

_____

_____

_____

FORGIVE ONE ANOTHER – EPHESIANS 4:32

_____

_____

_____

FOLLOW THE GOLDEN RULE – MATTHEW 7:12

_____

_____

_____

BRIGHT IDEA: Try putting these scriptures (and others) on a dry erase board one at a time in full view of the family. During breakfast or dinner, let your kids take turns reading the verses aloud and reciting them from memory. You can ask them simple questions about each verse to make sure they understand its meaning. This is a great way to hide the Word in their hearts!

A PAGE FROM THE PLAYBOOK

"It's easier to put a child's toys away than it is to teach him to put them away. It's easier to clean up a child's mess than it is to teach the child to clean up his own mess. However, if you take the easy way, your child doesn't acquire the skills he needs for common tasks around the house and you wind up taking care of him long after he should be able to care for himself.

...With younger children you can begin by having them pick up things with you—toys, clothes, papers, leaves. Show them where you want the things put. Older children can learn more complex tasks—setting the table, doing the dishes, running the vacuum, dusting the furniture, making beds, carrying out the garbage, mowing the grass, washing and drying clothes. Let them do these things with you or for you."

—Dr. Richard Dobbins[5]

(6) Getting kids to pitch in around the house can be challenging but it is important. It helps them learn responsibility and cooperation and gives them training for the real world. Take a few moments to jot down your children's chores, separating the daily ones (morning and night) from the weekly.

MORNING CHORES (ROUTINE THINGS TO DO BEFORE SCHOOL)

_____

_____

_____

_____

_____

_____

Include things like getting dressed, brushing teeth, fixing the bed, eating breakfast, etc.

EVENING CHORES (ROUTINE THINGS TO DO BEFORE GOING TO BED)

_____

_____

_____

_____

_____

Include things like doing homework, taking a bath, cleaning their room, setting the table, washing the dishes, etc.

WEEKLY CHORES (ROUTINE THINGS TO DO ON SET DAYS OF THE WEEK)

_____

_____

_____

_____

_____

Include things like taking out the trash, bathing the dog, cutting the grass, emptying the dishwasher, folding the clothes etc.

Post your child's chore list in their room. If your kids are small, take pictures of what their room, bathroom, etc., looks like clean and post them on the wall. This way they will know your expectations and have a specific goal to aim for. Periodically go over their chore list with them as well as the privileges they earn for a job well done. You may want to include a list of these privileges near the chore chart. This will definitely be a motivating force. And by all means, remember to reward approximations to success.

Something to Think About

The Rich Rewards of Routine

A *routine* is any activity that we do automatically on a regular basis. Children who grow up without routines, duties and boundaries, grow up in an uncontrolled manner and become difficult to manage. Routines can be established for everyday activities, household chores, and family fun time and devotions.

Routines...

♦ Help children feel safe and secure.

♦ Teach kids healthy habits, like brushing teeth, exercising, and washing hands after using the bathroom.

♦ Increase order and peace in the home; decrease stress and chaos.

♦ Help set our "body clocks" to instinctively know when it's time to go to sleep.

♦ Strengthen relationships between parents and children, especially those focused on fun, play, or quality time together.

♦ Enable everyone in the home to accomplish more through discipline.

According to the Center on the Social and Emotional Foundations for Early Learning, *Studies have documented that schedules and routines influence children's emotional, cognitive, and social development. Predictable and consistent schedules in preschool classrooms help children feel secure and comfortable. Also, schedules and routines help children understand the expectations of the environment and reduce the frequency of behavior problems, such as tantrums and acts of aggression.*[6]

SENSEI SAYS...

"Do you have trouble getting your kids to do chores? Tie a special privilege to each task. For instance, tell them, 'Once your room is cleaned, you can go ride your bike,' or play a video game or go by a friend's house or watch TV. Doing their chores and obeying the house rules earns them special privileges."

—Mike Storms

(7) In order to motivate our kids to carry out a specific task or move in a specific direction, we must help them stay *focused*. How do we help our kids stay focused? By eliminating as many distractions from their life as possible.

(a) Name the three biggest distractions in *your* life— things you know in your heart rob you of quality time with God, your spouse, and your children.

_____

_____

_____

(b) Now name the three biggest distractions in your *children's* lives.

CHILD 1 _____

_____

_____

_____

CHILD 2 _____

_____

_____

_____

CHILD 3 _____

_____

_____

_____

(c) Get quiet before God and ask Him to show you some
practical ways to eliminate these distractions from
your life and your children's lives. Write what He
reveals.

_____

_____

_____

TRUE STORY:

"COMING INTO FOCUS"

One of the things I hear from parents over and over again is,
"My kid doesn't listen." The truth is, kids don't automatically
listen, they must be *trained* to listen. This reminds me of a situation one of the families that attended our "Parenting
Bootcamp" shared with us awhile back—a situation we have
run across repeatedly. The mother said, "My daughter just
can't seem to focus; she's distracted. What can I do to help her
become more focused?"

I began asking some key questions. First, I asked her to tell me
about her daughter's schedule. It really wasn't too bad, but it
did reveal a couple of things. She was watching a little too
much TV, which will definitely hinder a child's ability to focus.
And she was also doing her homework after dinner, which is
rather late in the day. The best time to do homework is right

after school. Things are still fresh in kids' minds and they haven't gotten involved in anything else yet.

Next, I asked her to describe her daughter's room. This was the real eye-opener. Her room, as I suspected, was filled with numerous sources of distraction. Nowadays, kids' bedrooms are little dens. They often have a TV with a DVD player, video games, computer, and a stereo, not to mention a cell phone. It's no wonder they can't focus! As I gently pointed this out to both the mom and dad, they realized that their daughter could not possibly focus in that room. Consequently, they removed all the recreational electronics and her grades immediately went up.

I have hundreds of stories like this, including situations in which children with cell phones were constantly talking or texting at night. Once the phones were taken away, their grades went up. My point is, to motivate kids to focus, you must eliminate distractions. Limit the time they spend watching TV and playing video games; keep these activities in the den as they should be. This will help them focus and have better con-centration and performance in school.

AGELESS ADVICE

"Let us think of ways to **motivate** one another to acts of love and good works."

—**Hebrews 10:24 NLT**

A Page from the Playbook

"When motivating a child by using his or her 'natural bent' it is important to learn the child's *basic interests* and *talents*. You can use this knowledge to motivate that child to be a better student, eat healthier foods, read books, and do many other things. ...When parents use their children's interests to motivate them, the resulting progress is often amazing. Motivating a child through his interests is effective because it comes from within him. It reflects his bent."

—Gary Smalley[7]

(8) *Rewards* are powerful motivators for our kids to do the right thing—especially rewards that are linked to things they like and are interested in. Scripture says that "Blessings crown the head of the righteous..." (Proverbs 10:6 NIV). Would you like your kids to begin taking the *initiative* to do things without being asked? Then get creative! Make up some "Wanted" posters and put them up around the house. Write what you WANT to see them do along with the REWARD they'll receive for taking the initiative to do it.

Example 1: WANTED: Kid caught in a random act of kindness to his kin (sibling).

REWARD: You choose the movie everyone watches.

OR

You get the first piece of pie or cake.

Example 2: WANTED: Kid caught cleaning up to help his kin (parent or sibling).

REWARD: You choose the restaurant the family goes to on our next outing.

OR

Play a board game of your choice with Mom/Dad.

MY WANTED & REWARD POSTERS

WANTED: _____

REWARD: _____

WANTED: _____

REWARD: _____

WANTED: _____

REWARD: _____

WANTED: _____

REWARD: _____

WANTED: _____

REWARD: _____

Write 'em down and post 'em up! Make it fun, fresh, and interesting by putting up a poster in each room of the house and changing the rewards every other month or so.

AGELESS ADVICE

"...Write the vision and engrave it so plainly upon tablets that everyone who passes may [be able to] read [it easily and quickly] as he hastens by."

—Habakkuk 2:2 AMP

(9) If what you're doing to motivate your kids is not working, it's time to try something new. One inspiring exercise you can implement is *reminding them of their past successes*. In the space below, jot down some tough situations they have overcome and connect them to the challenge they are currently facing. This will help instill in them a sense of confidence and hope for victory.

SOME OF MY CHILD'S PAST SUCCESSES ARE...

_____

_____

_____

_____

_____

A PAGE FROM THE PLAYBOOK

"The line of dots that run up our wall

Tell us our child is growing quite tall;

Shoes that were too large now squeeze her toes,

My how quickly a little child grows.

We are so eager to keep track of her height,

In her physical growth we take such delight;

but spiritual growth, which to God is a treasure,

We might forget, and fail to measure."

—**Margaret Fishback Powers**[8]

(10) Last, but not least, how connected are your kids to God? Having a personal *relationship* with the Creator of heaven

and earth is the greatest motivating force in your children's lives. If you will do your part and help cultivate their relationship with God, He will continue to motivate them to live right throughout their entire lives.

(a) Does God want to be in relationship with kids as much as adults?

_____

_____

_____

Check out Matthew 19:13-15; Joel 2:28.

(b) What must your kids do to be in relationship with Him and receive His gift of salvation?

_____

_____

_____

Check out Romans 10:9,10.

(c) What happens in your children's lives when they invite God in and follow Him?

_____

_____

_____

Check out John 14:23; Revelation 3:20; 1 John 3:24.

(d) Can your children, who are in relationship with God, hear His voice motivating them?

_____

_____

_____

Check out 1 Samuel 3:1-10; John 10:4,5, 27.

Time to Reflect

SENSEI SAYS...

"Our kids are our responsibility. It's *not* the job of the teachers at school to teach our kids—it's our job. It's our job to make sure they are learning our values as well as our principles of success, nutrition, health, attitude, behavior, and character."

—**Mike Storms**

The list of creative ways to teach and motivate our children is seemingly unending. Ask the Lord to show you what is going to work best for each of your children at their individual age and situation. He knew each of them before He formed and "wired" them in the womb (see Jeremiah 1:5). Consequently, He knows exactly what is needed to motivate them to do right.

Take time now to write down the most eye-opening things you learned from this week's lesson.

_____

_____

_____

_____

_____

_____

_____

_____

---

(1) James C. Dobson, *The New Dare to Discipline* (Wheaton, IL: Tyndale House Publishers, Inc., 1992) pp.79-80. (2) Dr. Kevin Leman & Randy Carlson, *Parent Talk* (Nashville, TN: Thomas Nelson Publishers, 1993) p. 295. (3) Charles Stanley, *How to Keep Your Kids on Your Team* (Nashville, TN, Oliver-Nelson Books, a division of Thomas Nelson, Inc. Publishers, 1986) pp. 41-42. (4) Zig Ziglar, *Something to Smile About* (Nashville TN: Thomas Nelson, Inc., 1997) p. 93. (5) Dr. Richard Dobbins, *Venturing Into a Child's World* (Old Tappan, NJ: Fleming H. Revell Company, 1985) p. 123. (6) *The Importance of Teaching Children Routines* (www.milestoneparenting.com/productinfo/ImportanceOfRoutines.aspx, retrieved 5-18-10). (7) Gary Smalley, *The Key to Your Child's Heart* (Dallas, TX: Word Publishing, 1992) pp. 150-151. (8) *365 Day Brighteners Celebrating Mothers* (Siloam Springs, AR: Garborg's®, A brand of Dayspring® Cards, Inc., 2005) July 29.

Chapter 6

How to Avoid Eight Common Parenting Pitfalls

"Why not bite off a chunk of time during the next few months for a single purpose—to evaluate the present condition of your home and then to set in motion the necessary steps needed to strengthen the weaknesses you uncover.

...Use this period of time as an opportunity to get next to your children...to come to grips with the barriers that are blocking the flow of your love and affection (and theirs)...to evaluate how much character development is going on...to face the facts before the nagging sore spots lead to a permanent, domestic disease. Guard your heart from negligence!"

—Charles R. Swindoll[1]

Chapter 6
How to Avoid Eight Common Parenting Pitfalls

Please refer to Chapter 6 in the *Parenting 101* book along with Session 6 of the CD series.

SENSEI SAYS...

"When correcting your kids, don't embitter them. Give them discipline, but do it calmly, not in anger. Remember, when rapport is broken, teaching stops."

—Mike Storms

AGELESS ADVICE

"He who is slow to anger is better than the mighty, and he who rules his spirit, than he who captures a city."
—Proverbs 16:32 NASB

(1) One of the biggest pitfalls parents face is *yelling* at their kids and correcting them in anger. As we learned in chapter 4, anger does *not* produce the righteousness, or right behavior, in our children that God wants and we want. Therefore, we have to learn to stay calm, cool, and in control.

(a) Name the number one thing that each of your children does that causes you to explode in anger.

CHILD 1 _____ - _____

CHILD 2 _____ - _____

CHILD 3 _____ - _____

(b) Do you have *set consequences* for these behaviors? If so, what are they? Have you followed through quickly with the consequences? If not, why?

_____

_____

_____

Note: We often blow up because we have not followed through quickly and calmly with the consequences we've established. Consistent, quick discipline delivered in a calm way is the key to healthy, effective correction.

(c) Many times explosive anger is the visible fruit of a deeper root. Get quiet before God and ask Him to show you *why* you explode in anger; ask Him to forgive you and give you His strength and a practical plan to bring about change. Write what He reveals and then go to the child who observed your explosion and seek forgiveness.

_____

_____

_____

AGELESS ADVICE

"Investigate my life, O God, find out everything about me; cross-examine and test me, get a clear picture of what I'm about; see for yourself whether I've done anything wrong—then guide me on the road to eternal life."
—Psalm 139:23,24 The Message

A PAGE FROM THE PLAYBOOK

"Getting angry and yelling all kinds of unreasonable threats diminishes our children's respect for us. So it is important to remember that *we must not get out of control while trying to bring our children under control.* ...If your children learn that they can drive you to acting worse than they do, they will delight in doing so. However, displaying controlled anger to your children lets them know you are displeased and that you mean business. When they are convinced that you really mean what you say, they will gain new respect for you."

—**Joyce Meyer**[2]

---

(2) Arguing, or quarrelling, with our kids, is always a "lose-lose" situation and a pitfall we definitely need to avoid. Even if we win the fight, we may end up losing the war because of the deadly disease of *strife* that we let into our relationships.

    (a) According to Proverbs 15:18, 17:19 and 29:22, what kind of attitude gives birth to strife? What do these verses say to you?

       _____

       _____

       _____

    (b) It's clear in scripture that God does *not* want us to argue or quarrel. *Write* out and commit to memory these two key verses.

       PHILIPPIANS 2:14

       _____

       _____

       _____

2 TIMOTHY 2:24

_____

_____

_____

(c) Many problems caused by strife can be prevented by taking the high road of *humility*. *Read* these verses and *write* the **blessings** that come from being humble: Psalm 18:27; 25:9; Proverbs 18:12; 22:4; 29:23; James 4:6; 1 Peter 5:5.

THE BLESSINGS OF BEING HUMBLE ARE:

_____

_____

_____

AGELESS ADVICE

"...Clothe (apron) yourselves, all of you, with *humility* [as the garb of a servant, so that its covering cannot possibly be stripped from you, with freedom from pride and arrogance] toward one another. For God sets Himself against the proud (the insolent, the overbearing, the disdainful, the presumptuous, the boastful)—[and He opposes, frustrates, and defeats them], but gives grace (favor, blessing) to the humble."

—1 Peter 5:5 AMP

SENSEI SAYS...

"Don't *over explain* everything to your children. Over-explaining partners with their disobedience. You can't put a thirty- or forty-year-old head on a five-year-old body. They are just not going to understand everything, and they don't have to. They need to obey."

—Mike Storms

(3) Next to arguing with our kids is the habit of *over explaining* ourselves. It is true that as our children get older, we should share with them the purpose behind their punishment. But even then, we must use wisdom and not do it every time.

(a) Do you have a tendency to over explain things to your children? If so, why?

_____

_____

_____

(b) Many times the root reason for over explaining is *insecurity*—a fear of being rejected by our kids or being too hard or being an inadequate parent. Can you identify with any of these? Explain.

_____

_____

_____

(4) Parenting our kids out of *fear* is another common pitfall to avoid. Many times fear connected with pain from our childhood subtly dictates the way we discipline our kids. With God's help, we can learn to discern these unhealthy patterns and replace them.

(a) Were you wounded as a child by correction you received? If so, describe what happened.

_____

_____

_____

(b) How is that experience affecting the way you raise your kids today?

_____

_____

_____

(c) Have you ever corrected (or not corrected) your children out of fear that they would experience the pain that you experienced as a child? Explain the situation.

_____

_____

_____

A PAGE FROM THE PLAYBOOK

"...Moms can be controlled by fear, too. We're afraid our kids will get hurt on the merry-go-round, so we focus on their grip rather than their grin. We don't let them make mud cakes, worried about some sinister bacteria. Our worst fear is that we will somehow fail as mothers. Fear can consume our thoughts; what we've known to be true, such as the goodness and faithfulness of God, can become gray or forgotten. ...Fear pulls us from God when we resort to our own limited ability rather than His unlimited resources. And He allows us to pull away until, exhausted, we're finally ready to trust Him."

—Simone Devon-Lee[3]

(5) Insecurity, inferiority, doubt, anxiety, worry, and people pleasing are forms of fear that are sometimes hard to detect. In any case, if our actions are motivated by fear, we open the door to the enemy to bring problems into our lives and the lives of our children.

(a) Have you ever corrected your kids because you were embarrassed by their behavior? How is this reaction connected with fear?

_____

_____

(b) Have you ever *withheld* correction out of fear of your child's reaction? What were you trying to avoid? What happened as a result? _____

_____

_____

_____

(c) Take a moment to pray and ask God to show you any area of your parenting where fear is motivating you. Write what He shows you and surrender it to Him.

_____

_____

_____

Instead of being motivated by fear, God wants us to be motivated by faith. In other words, when we bring correction to our kids, we believe what we are doing and saying to them is the right and best thing for their overall well-being.

AGELESS ADVICE

"Let your *Yes* be simply Yes, and your *No* be simply No; anything more than that comes from the evil one."
—**Matthew 5:37 AMP**

A PAGE FROM THE PLAYBOOK

"Threatening our children or employees is evidence of a lack of true authority. The rewards and penalties should already be clear, and if there is disobedience, discipline should be administered the *first time*, not further threatening. If we have to threaten to compel our children or anyone else that we are in charge of to obey us, then somehow it has already been established that our 'yes' did not really mean 'yes,' and our 'no' did not really mean 'no.'"
—**Rick Joyner**[4]

(6) Another common mistake I see parents make is threatening their kids with consequences for wrong behavior and then not following through. Instead of doing this, we need to *say what we mean and mean what we say.* Think for a moment...

(a) What unspoken message are you sending to your kids when you threaten to punish them for bad behavior but only sporadically follow through with consequences?

_____

_____

_____

(b) Why is counting to three every time your child misbehaves *not* a constructive, positive way to teach your children? _____

_____

_____

_____

(c) Did your parents threaten you when you were growing up? If so, did it work? How did it make you feel? What does your experience say to you regarding your kids?

_____

_____

_____

Remember, give your kids *open-ended consequences.* Tell them, "You'll get your TV (or telephone, video games, friends, etc.) privileges back when your behavior changes." This motivates them to really look at their behavior and choose to change it.

SENSEI SAYS...

"Our kids are *not* on equal footing with us. We are the generals; they are the privates. While generals certainly argue with generals, they don't argue with privates or lieutenants. Don't *negotiate* with your kids. We only negotiate with peers and people on the same level."

—Mike Storms

(7) Some well-meaning parents migrate toward the pitfall of trying to be their child's best friend. Your kids have friends; it is parents that they need. God has selected you to fill that role. Realize that if you exchange your role as parent for being their best friend, you abdicate your position of protection and leadership and leave them vulnerable.

(a) Are there certain areas in any of your children's lives where you would rather be their best friend instead of their parent? If so, what areas?

_____

_____

_____

(b) What is the motivating, root reason you want to be their best friend instead of their parent?

_____

_____

_____

This is a good place to pause and pray; ask God to reveal to you the motives of your heart.

(c) In view of what God has revealed, what adjustments can you make to overcome this pitfall? Again, ask God for His input.

_____

_____

_____

A Page from the Playbook

"Some parents have abdicated their role and have withdrawn from even the proper use of authority. ...God has established the institution of the parent as one of His ruling authorities on earth. To this position has been delegated both the right to rule children and all the power necessary to succeed in training children according to God's plan. This position is the direct agency through which children are to receive ruling during their childhood. That is, it is through this position that each child is to receive protection, direction, and instruction."

—J. Richard Fugate[5]

(8) Parents who surrender their position of authority over their children often fall into another common snare—they *ask* their children to do things instead of *telling* them to.

(a) How often does the phrase "Will you do this" come out of your mouth when you are trying to motivate your kids to do things—sometimes, all the time, seldom, or never?

_____

_____

_____

(b) Stop and ask yourself, "*Why* do I ask my kids to do things instead of tell them—what is motivating me?"

_____

_____

_____

(c) If you are *asking* your kids to do things more often than *telling* them, how are they responding? Do you see a difference from when you tell them to do something? If so, what is it?

_____

_____

_____

(9) It is clear from the examples in Scripture that God does not want us to water down our discipline. Our words are to be spoken in love, but they are also to be firm. *Read* God's judgment against Eli and his sons in 2 Samuel 2:12-36 and 3:11-14.

(a) In light of these verses, how important to God is giving your kids solid, straightforward correction?

_____

_____

_____

(b) *Reread* 1 Samuel 2:29 and 3:13 and identify what Eli's (the parent) sin was.

_____

_____

_____

(c) What does this example from Scripture speak to you about parenting your children?

_____

_____

AGELESS ADVICE

"Don't fail to discipline your children. They won't die if you spank them. Physical discipline may well save them from death."

—Proverbs 23:13,14 NLT

(10) Another common pitfall parents experience is *over commitment*—allowing their children to participate in <u>too</u> many activities at once, or over committed to <u>one</u> activity. As a result, many moms end up playing taxi driver all week long and living stressed-out lives.

(a) How many clubs, sports, or extracurricular activities are your kids presently involved in?

CHILD 1 _____ CHILD 2 _____ CHILD 3 _____

(b) Choosing one or two activities (no more than three) is a more balanced, less stressful approach. List the top three activities for each of your children—things they enjoy most and are good at.

CHILD 1 _____ CHILD 2 _____ CHILD 3 _____

1) _____ 1) _____ 1) _____

2) _____ 2) _____ 2) _____

3) _____ 3) _____ 3) _____

(c) What are the benefits of letting your children try different sports and activities until they are about seven or eight? Why is it important to make them focus on one or two things after that age?

_____

_____

_____

A PAGE FROM THE PLAYBOOK

"If you fill your children's schedule with Scouts, piano lessons, soccer leagues, and Awana club, you could be flirting with burnout for them—and *yourself*. Just as you have to learn to say no to opportunities in your own life, so you will have to say no for your kid. Some children will be able to handle a lot more than others. Find your children's stamina level, but don't exceed it. No matter how energetic your kids are, every school afternoon shouldn't be taken up with activities. Children need unstructured time to goof off with their friends."

—Greg Johnson and Mike Yorkey[6]

(11) Maybe you are struggling with a different pitfall that has not been mentioned. If so, briefly describe what it is. Retrace your steps in your relationship with your child and try to pinpoint when this problem first began. Pray and ask God to show you the root cause of the situation and how to overcome it. Write what He reveals.

_____

_____

_____

SENSEI SAYS...

"You don't have to be a perfect parent. I am not a perfect parent. Ask my kids, my wife, or anybody else who knows me. The thing is, you don't have to be perfect to succeed—you just need to be trying, learning, growing, and making better decisions."

—Mike Storms

Something to Think About

If a child lives with *criticism*, he learns to condemn.

If a child lives with *hostility*, he learns to fight.

If a child lives with *fear*, he learns to be apprehensive.

If a child lives with *pity*, he learns to feel sorry for himself.

If a child lives with *jealousy*, he learns to feel guilty.

If a child lives with *encouragement*, he learns to be self-confident.

If a child lives with *tolerance*, he learns to be patient.

If a child lives with *praise*, he learns to be appreciative.

If a child lives with *acceptance*, he learns to love.

If a child lives with *approval*, he learns to like himself.

If a child lives with *recognition*, he learns to have a goal.

If a child lives with *fairness*, he learns what justice is.

If a child lives with *honesty*, he learns what truth is.

If a child lives with *sincerity*, he learns to have faith in himself and those around him.

If a child lives with *love*, he learns that the world is a wonderful place to live in.[7]

TRUE STORY:

"DON'T BE AFRAID TO ESTABLISH BOUNDARIES"

I've seen it hundreds of times before. Parents who are afraid of how their children will respond to firm rules and boundaries. Parents who fear the loss of the approval of their children more than they fear what will happen to their children's characters without these boundaries. Even parents held hostage by fear of how their children will behave in public.

Studies show, over and over again that consistent, communicated and enforced boundaries make kids feel safe and even develop their confidence in themselves.

Like most parents, my wife and I established a curfew for our teenaged sons while they were in high school based on their age and responsibility level. The rule was - you break the curfew, you lose your driving privileges for the next weekend.

As it often does, the first test of our resolve came quickly. One of my sons, for no reason whatsoever arrived home thirty minutes late. His excuse was that he got lost driving a friend home, caught all the lights, yada, yada, yada. "No big deal, Dad. It wasn't my fault."

The following weekend was the homecoming dance. My son had some pretty big plans with a lovely young lady. At this point, I had two choices: I could do what I said I would do when we established the rules and punish him no matter how much it hurt us both, or go easy on him because it was the first time, it was only thirty minutes, it wasn't his fault and all the other excuses I thought of to justify not having to this thing I did not want to do. I feared my son's wrath and his possible hatred of me.

"I understand, son." I said. "Give me the keys to your car." Then he began to plead. "Dad you're not going to make me miss homecoming are you?" "No, you aren't going to miss it, but you aren't going to drive."

The following weekend, I drove my son and his date to the homecoming dance. Was he angry? Yes, but he got over it and I did not tolerate any hostile behavior from him. That week I spent more time with him , just talking and building our relationship even closer. It was important for him to know that even though I enforced consequences, I still loved him.

Needless to say, we did not have another curfew issue for a very long time. I know that if I had let it slide and allowed him to drive to homecoming because it was a "special night" or "no big deal", it would have been the beginning of many more tests. By not consistently enforcing our rules with consequences, we are training our children to misbehave, to take a chance because sometimes the gamble pays off.

Another benefit to enforcing rules is that your other children are learning through observation. Do you think my other son ever broke his curfew? Not once. He learned through his brother's actions and consequences.

I love my kids, therefore I owe it to them to train them that actions have consequences, no matter how it makes them feel about me.

Time to Reflect

Let's review the Eight Common Pitfalls of Parenting we want to avoid:

1) Don't yell at your kids and correct them out of anger; stay calm, cool, and in control.

2) Avoid arguing, or quarrelling, with your kids; it opens the door to the deadly disease of strife.

3) Don't over explain everything to your children. Over-explaining partners with their disobedience.

4) Steer clear of being fearful in any form.

5) Avoid threatening your kids with consequences and not following through. Be consistent.

6) Don't try to be your child's best friend. Friends they have; it is parents that they need.

7) Don't *ask* your kids to do things; take the leadership role and *tell* them what to do.

8) Avoid over commitment. Choose one or two sports or activities your kids enjoy and are good at.

Take a moment to jot down anything God is showing you through this lesson. What scriptures really came alive that you want to commit to memory? What principles helped you see a side of yourself you have never seen before? Reflecting on the truth that God shows you in His Word and in your life is what sets you free.

_____

_____

_____

---

(1) Charles R. Swindoll, *The Quest for Character* (Portland, OR; Multnomah Press, 1987) p. 104. (2) Joyce Meyer, "Discovering God's Divine Plan for Parenting" (*Enjoying Everyday Life* magazine, August 2004, Joyce Meyer Ministries, Inc., Fenton, MO 63026) p.7. (3) Simone Devon-Lee, "Consumed by Fear" (*Focus on the Family* magazine, August 2008, Colorado Springs, CO 80920) p. 13. (4) Quotes on *Children & Family* (http://dailychristian quote.com/dcqfamily.html, retrieved 4/29/10). (5) J. Richard Fugate, *What the Bible Says About Child Training* (Apache Junction, AZ: Foundation for Biblical Research, 1996) pp. 31, 38. (6) Greg Johnson and Mike Yorkey, *Faithful Parents, Faithful Kids* (Wheaton, IL: Tyndale House Publishers, Inc., 1993) p. 63. (7) Illustrations on *Parenting* (http://www.sermonillustrations.com /a-z/p/parenting.htm, retrieved 6-10-10).

Chapter 7

Developing Seven Characteristics of an All-Star Parent

"...There is no right or wrong parenting style. The only real qualification that parents need is a sincere and diligent desire to follow God's ways. God knew your strengths and weaknesses when you signed up to be a parent, and He still hired you. So if He doesn't regret giving you the job of raising His children, then you have nothing to feel guilty about. You are free to be yourself. You know your kids and what they need, so trust the insight God has given you. He assures us in 2 Corinthians 12:9-10 that He will be strong where we are weak. All we have to do is depend on Him."

—Lisa Whelchel[1]

Chapter 7

Developing Seven Characteristics of an All-Star Parent

Please refer to Chapter 7 in the *Parenting 101* book along with Session 7 of the CD series.

SENSEI SAYS...

"Parents, develop a strong spiritual foundation in your children. There are certain things you have in your house that are non-negotiable, and this should be one of them. Regardless of any resistance, choose to say as Joshua said, '...As for me and my house, we will serve the Lord' (Joshua 24:15 NKJV)."

—**Mike Storms**

(1) The most important quality of an all-star parent is a strong spiritual foundation—in *your* life and in *your children's* lives. If you are connected in an ongoing, personal relationship with God, building a spiritual foundation in your kids will come naturally.

(a) According to **Psalm 78:1-8**...

What does God want you to share with your children? Is this a suggestion?

_____

_____

_____

Check out verse 5.

For what reasons does He want you to share this with them?

_____

_____

_____

Check out verses 6 and 7.

What does He *not* want to happen to them?

_____

_____

_____

Check out verse 8.

(b) Carefully *read* **Deuteronomy 6:4-9** and answer the following questions.

In God's eyes, how important is it to teach His words of instruction to your family?

_____

_____

_____

How often does He want you to share them with your children?

_____

_____

_____

In your own words, what do you think He is saying to us today in verses 8 and 9?

_____

_____

_____

A Page from the Playbook

"A strong *spiritual foundation* is essential for healthy children, families and society. Children who have a healthy spiritual foundation grow up knowing they are loved by their Creator, who has endowed them with unique gifts, talents and abilities. When children have a personal connection with God and know what the Bible says about them, they are better equipped to accurately assess their abilities and live life to the fullest."

—Dr. Walt Larimore[2]

(2) Do you know the spiritual "pulse" of your family? Answer these six questions to reveal...

Your Family's Spiritual Vital Signs

- How often does the subject of God, Jesus, or something from the Bible come up in conversation? Would you say daily, weekly, monthly, yearly, or hardly ever?

  _____

  _____

  _____

- Do you read the Bible or go over scriptures together as a family? If so, how often?

  _____

  _____

  _____

- Do you pray together as a family? If so, how often?

  _____

  _____

  _____

- Do you go to church together? If so, how often?

  _____

  _____

  _____

- Review your answers. What do your family's spiritual vital signs say to you? Would you like to see them change? If yes, what would you like them to be?

  _____

  _____

  _____

Commit your desire for a spiritually healthy family to the Lord. Pray and ask Him to bless your family with a fresh desire to know and serve Him. Also, ask Him to show you how to weave His Word into your daily conversations and apply it to everyday situations. The results will be life-changing!

SENSEI SAYS...

"Make it a priority to *study* how to be a good parent. I make it a point to read a parenting book every month. I'm on parenting websites every week, reading blogs and finding things to implement in order to help counsel and coach the parents I'm working with, not to mention improve my own parenting."

—Mike Storms

(3) More than likely you have purchased resources, have magazine subscriptions, and have attended workshops to help you increase your level of excellence at your job or with a hobby. Similarly, studying to improve as a parent is just as important—actually it's more important. It is another characteristic of an all-star parent.

(a) What have you bought, borrowed, or done to better yourself as a parent? Of these, which things would you recommend to a friend? Why?

_____

_____

_____

These things include purchasing or borrowing books, CDs, DVDs, and attending special training classes or seminars.

(b) If you have not purchased, borrowed, or checked out from the library any resources, why? Can you now see the importance and value of doing this?

_____

_____

_____

AGELESS ADVICE

"Study to shew thyself approved unto God, a workman that needeth not to be ashamed, rightly dividing the word of truth."

—2 Timothy 2:15 KJV

(4)   The Bible is the ultimate book to study for all-star parenting. It is filled with examples of both good parents and not so good parents. Of all the real-life examples, who do you most want to be like? Why? Who do you least want to be like? Why?

THE BIBLICAL CHARACTER I *MOST* ADMIRE AND WANT TO IMITATE IS...

_____

_____

THE BIBLICAL CHARACTER I *LEAST* ADMIRE AND DO NOT WANT TO IMITATE IS...

_____

_____

_____

(5) Another source of help in our parenting is the godly people God has placed around us. Indeed, as parents we should never "go it alone" but seek the counsel of others—those who have blazed the trail before us and have successfully raised their children past the ages and stages of ours.

(a) According to God's Word, why is it important to seek counsel? What often keeps us from doing it?

_____

_____

_____

Check out Proverbs 11:14; 12:15; 13:10; 15:22.

(b) Who do you turn to for wisdom and advice when it comes to parenting? Why?

_____

_____

_____

AGELESS ADVICE

"Plans fail for lack of counsel, but with many advisers they succeed."

—Proverbs 15:22 NIV

SENSEI SAYS...

"Parenting is not a popularity contest. Don't be swayed by the opinions of your parents, grandparents, coworkers, or friends. Don't let people dictate how you parent by worrying about their opinion of you. Their opinion doesn't matter. Do what you know is right and best for your kids."

—Mike Storms

(6) While we should seek wise counsel, we must also guard against becoming overly concerned with what everybody thinks of us. *People pleasing*, which the Bible calls the fear of man, can become quite a snare. But as all-star parents we can become immune to the criticism of others by submitting to God and receiving His help.

(a) Arrange these people in order of whose opinion is *most important* to you (be honest): your parents, friends, neighbors, pastor, coworkers, and God.

_____

_____

_____

If God is not first, do you know why? Ask Him to show you your heart.

(b) What happens when you build up an *immunity* to something? What do you think is involved with becoming immune to the criticism of others?

_____

_____

_____

126

(c) *Write* out and hide in your heart these powerful principles about who we should fear.

ISAIAH 8:13

_____

_____

_____

PROVERBS 29:25

_____

_____

_____

AGELESS ADVICE

"All has been heard; the end of the matter is: Fear God [revere and worship Him, knowing that He is] and keep His commandments, for this is the whole of man [the full, original purpose of his creation, the object of God's providence, the root of character, the foundation of all happiness, the adjustment to all inharmonious circumstances and conditions under the sun] and the whole [duty] for every man."
—**Ecclesiastes 12:13 AMP**

A PAGE FROM THE PLAYBOOK

"It is only the fear of God that can deliver us from the fear of man."
—**John Witherspoon**[3]

(7) Few stories in scripture illustrate the grave danger of disobedience and fearing what people think like the story of King Saul and his assignment to destroy the Amalekites. *Read* 1 Samuel 15:1-30 and answer the following questions.

(a) According to verses 22-24, what did the fear of others cause Saul to do?

_____

_____

_____

(b) How important do you think *obedience* is to God?

_____

_____

_____

(c) What other major character flaw caused Saul to do what he did?

_____

_____

_____

Check out verse 12 for a major clue.

(d) What does this example speak to you regarding what others think about the way you raise and discipline your children?

_____

_____

_____

AGELESS ADVICE

"Listen with *respect* to the father who raised you, and when your mother grows old, don't neglect her. Buy truth—don't sell it for love or money; buy wisdom, buy education, buy insight. Parents rejoice when their children turn out well; wise children become proud parents. So make your father happy! Make your mother proud!"

—Proverbs 23:22-25 The Message

(8) Another vital quality of an all-star parent is choosing to give up being *liked* by your kids in exchange for being *respected* by them. What is respect? It is to honor, value, and attach worth to.

(a) Why do you think it is more important to be respected than liked by your children?

_____

_____

_____

(b) What kind of things do you think make your kids respect you? How about *not* respect you?

_____

_____

_____

Hint: What kind of things did your parents (or people in authority) do that made you respect them? What made you not respect them? These things give you a good place to start.

(c) If you are feeling brave and want some honest feedback, ask your kids to complete these sentences:

"The thing I love and respect most about Mom/Dad is..."

_____

_____

_____

"If I could change one thing about Mom/Dad to make me respect them more, it would be..."

_____

_____

_____

A PAGE FROM THE PLAYBOOK

"What do you first envision when you think of respect? High regard for those in authority? Honor for the elderly? Maybe esteem for a person's noteworthy accomplishments or for his ability to persevere? ...There is something much deeper and inherently more central to the concept of respect: the glory of God imprinted into the essence of man. In encountering *any* person, we ought to marvel at all of the things that are good and admirable and beautiful about them (Philippians 4:8). ...We need to search for His glory in each individual until we find it, and then we need to celebrate it!"

—**Stephanie O. Hubach**[4]

(9) Recognizing bad behavior in all its forms and expecting obedience is also a valuable ability of an all-star parent. But how do we do this—how can we recognize when their attitudes and actions are not measuring up? We must have a standard of "right" that we can measure it against.

(a) Why would the standards presented in most of today's media not serve as a good measurement for our kids' behavior?

_____

_____

_____

(b) *Read* 2 Timothy 3:16,17, Psalm 119:89, and Matthew 24:35 and tell the one thing that you can always use to measure your children's conduct and why it is reliable.

_____

_____

_____

(b) There's one more thing that you need to accurately discern and effectively direct your kids' behavior. *Read* Nehemiah 9:20 and John 14:26 and 16:13 and identify this Helper and His job.

_____

_____

_____

A PAGE FROM THE PLAYBOOK

"Enjoy your kids. Let the sound of laughter ring through your house. Roughhouse when they're little, play board games, linger around the dinner table, roll on the grass, and thumb through your photo albums. Will creating an atmosphere of fun help your children be faithful kids? Maybe, maybe not, but the odds are weighted in your favor when you're fun to be around.

Think about it. What's really important? Answer: that your children come to know Christ and receive eternal salvation. If that's what you want for your children, and we're sure it is, then start building those relationships long before they pack their bags for college."

—Greg Johnson & Mike Yorkey[5]

(10) Creating fun-filled family moments and surprises are definitely a mark of an all-star parent. Having fun is really not about spending a lot of money. It's about generating laughter, love, and genuine joy within the family. So here's the question: What kind of things do your kids and spouse enjoy?

(a) Take a quick survey: Ask each family member to name three to five indoor or outdoor activities that they think are fun. Write down what they say.

MY FAMILY'S FEEDBACK ON HAVING FUN

Child 1_____Child 2 _____Child 3 _____

_____ _____ _____

_____ _____ _____

_____ _____ _____

_____ _____ _____

_____ _____ _____

Mom's Idea of Having Fun   Dad's Idea of Having Fun

_____   _____

_____   _____

_____   _____

_____   _____

_____   _____

_____   _____

(b) Think outside the box! Turn these *ordinary* situations into *extraordinary* situations.

Make your trip to the grocery store with the kids an enjoyable experience.

_____

_____

_____

Turn your Friday night monotony into a variety of vivacity!

_____

_____

_____

Your Saturday plans to picnic and play in the park are rained out. What indoor ideas can you put into motion to salvage the situation?

_____

_____

_____

BRIGHT IDEA: Get an old pickle jar or coffee can and make a label on it that says "Family *Fund* Night." Let the whole family freely pitch in their loose coins as they desire. Money collected can be used to make an impromptu ice cream run, movie rental, or special shopping spree at the dollar store. Remember, having fun doesn't necessarily mean spending a lot of money. It's togetherness that really counts.

SENSEI SAYS...

"Teach your kids the importance of family coming first. Say to them, 'In our family, we look out for and take care of each other; we protect our family name and don't broadcast all of our business.'"

—Mike Storms

(11) Appreciating and valuing our family members is another key characteristic of an all-star parent. This includes honoring those older, younger, and on the same level with us and developing a habit of looking out for each other.

(a) What things do you treasure most about your family heritage that you want to pass on to your children?

_____

_____

_____

(b) In what ways would you like your kids to look out for their siblings? And you? Have you communicated these desires to them?

_____

_____

_____

(c) Why is it important to keep family information confidential? Ask your children this question also and jot down their answers. If they are not sure or don't know, share your heart with them in a way they can understand.

_____

_____

_____

A PAGE FROM THE PLAYBOOK

"Brothers and sisters are a blessing to each other. You will have many different friends come and go through your life, but the one constant will be your family. You are walking through life together, so take care of each other and make it a pleasant journey."

—**Karen Santorum**[6]

(12) Make a brief list of five honorable acts your parents or grandparents did that you want your children to know about. These include heroic war stories, educational achievements, outstanding acts of community service, and other accounts from family history. If the family member is still alive and able to share their story with your children, by all means, set up a time to meet with them.

HONORABLE AND HEROIC ACTS I WANT MY CHILDREN TO KNOW INCLUDE...

1)_____

2)_____

3)_____

4)_____

5)_____

This list can be expanded and creatively used as story starters while driving in the car, sitting around the dinner table, or walking in the woods. You can also gather heroic stories of your spouse as well as aunts and uncles. They are a great way to bridge the gap between generations and create a deep appreciation for family.

SOMETHING TO THINK ABOUT

AN INDISPENSABLE INGREDIENT TO PRODUCING HAPPY, HEALTHY CHILDREN

"In a recent study at Boston University, researchers stumbled upon a child-rearing study based on interviews with mothers of kindergarten children in the early 1950s. They decided to follow up and see how the children were faring as adults. After locating and questioning 78 percent of the original group, they discovered that the happiest respondents—those who enjoyed their jobs and their families and had a zest for living—all showed one important characteristic: *their parents had been warm and affectionate, generous with hugs, kisses, and play time.* The most important predictor of future happiness was not a good education or an upscale home, but physical closeness with parents. Factors such as money, major injuries, or even frequent moves had much less bearing on a child's future happiness than genuine affection."[7]

TRUE STORY:

"ENDING THE BATTLE AMONG BROTHERS"

By now, after reading my story and listening to the CDs, you know that I have a fractured family. I do *not* call it a blended family for two reasons: first, it lessens the impact of what has been done; and second, I feel the term blended is a farce that enables people to feel better about getting divorced.

I have two kids from my first marriage, and my wife has one from hers. We also have one together. We were both divorced more than a decade before we came to know the Lord. Still in our parenting program, we had two sons from different houses that are one year apart. They were as different as could be—one was a genius and the other an athlete. In time, both became athletic and academic all-stars.

The first year or so after we got married, the boys got into some pretty serious fights. Consequently, I decided to remove all their privileges. It was then that I established my favorite consequence clause: "You are punished until further notice" or "until this improves." In other words, until they learned to get along, share, and be friendly, they would have no privileges whatsoever. Amazingly, in a matter of weeks, their relationship improved. We encouraged, coached, and taught them to treat each other right. Fifteen years have passed, and now at the ages of eighteen and nineteen, I'm glad to report that they are close friends. They actually hang out with each other and have chosen to do so for many years.

So when I hear a parent who has children that are fighting tell me, "That's just the way brothers and sisters are," I don't buy it. You shouldn't either. It's just an excuse to not address the problem. Don't tolerate fighting in your house—deal with it. Make your children treat each other, and you and your spouse, the way they treat their friends and other people they respect.

A couple more things: If you or your spouse have children from a previous marriage, do away with the word "stepchild." We never used that term....ever. It separates. Also, remember respect and good character is taught by example. If you fight and argue, so will your kids. Work on *you* first, and then the kids will follow. Make sure you are leading the way by your example.

Time to Reflect

Let's recap the 7 Characteristics of an All-Star Parent:

1) Develop a strong spiritual foundation—in your life and in your children's lives.

2) Continue to study and improve yourself as a parent; this includes seeking the counsel of others.

3) Escape the trap of people pleasing by becoming immune to the criticism of others.

4) Choose to give up being liked by your children in exchange for being respected by them.

5) Recognize bad behavior in all its forms and expect obedience.

6) Become an expert at creating fun-filled family moments and surprises.

7) Teach your children to appreciate and value family members and history.

Remember, becoming an all-star parent is a *process*—something we walk out one day at a time. Let the Lord, the greatest MVP coach of all time, show you how to apply these key principles daily and build happy, healthy children. Relax in your relationship with Him. He will prompt you on what to do!

Take a moment to jot down anything He is showing you through this lesson. It's worth the effort!

_____

_____

_____

_____

_____

_____

_____

_____

_____

_____

_____

_____

_____

_____

_____

_____

_____

_____

_____

_____

_____

_____

_____

_____

_____

(1) Lisa Whelchel, *Creative Correction* (Wheaton, IL: Tyndale House Publishers, Inc., 2005) p.132. (2) "The Antidote of Faith," by Dr. Walt Larimore (*Focus on the Family* magazine, January 2009, Colorado Springs, CO) pp. 22-23. (3) Christian Quotes on *Fear* (http://dailychristianquote. com/dcqfear2.html, retrieved 5/23/10). (4) "Reflecting God's Image," by Stephanie O. Hubach (*Focus on the Family* magazine, January 2009, Colorado Springs, CO) pp. 20-21.(5) Greg Johnson and Mike Yorkey, *Faithful Parents, Faithful Kids* (Wheaton, IL: Tyndale House Publishers, Inc., 1993) p. 307. (6) Karen Santorum, *Everyday Graces—A Child's Book of Good Manners* (Wilmington, DE: ISI Books, 2005) p. 29. (7) Stephen Arterburn & Jim Burns, *Parents Guide to Top 10 Dangers Teens Face* (Wheaton, IL, A Focus on the Family Book published by Tyndale House Publishers, 1995) pp. 282-283.

Chapter 8

Never Underestimate the Power of Prayer!

"We need to be able to pray. We need prayer just like we need air. Without prayer, we can do nothing.

...Jesus is always waiting for us in silence. In this silence He listens to us; it is there that He speaks to our souls. And there, we hear His voice."

—Mother Teresa[1]

Chapter 8

Never Underestimate the Power of Prayer!

Please refer to Chapter 8 in the *Parenting 101* book along with Session 8 of the CD series.

SENSEI SAYS...

"Pray for your kids *all the time*, whenever a situation arises. Pray for them in your private time; pray over them out loud at night for a peaceful night's rest. Pray for them to study and do well on their exams...pray for them to connect in healthy relationships, including their husband or wife to be."

—**Mike Storms**

(1) Many wonderful principles on parenting have been presented in the previous chapters. But without the wisdom and power of God to put them into practice, they will remain just that—wonderful principles. How do we receive His wisdom and power? By staying connected with Him in *prayer*.

(a) In your own words, describe what prayer means to you. How significant is it in your life?

_____

_____

_____

(b) Do you believe in the power of prayer—do you believe that God hears you when you pray and will answer your prayers? Why or why not?

_____

_____

(c) Carefully *read* these Scriptures and write down what they say to you regarding how God answers prayer.

MATTHEW 7:7-11 AND LUKE 11:9-12

_____

_____

_____

JOHN 14:12-14 AND MATTHEW 21:22

_____

_____

_____

AGELESS ADVICE

"Pray *all the time*. Ask God for anything in line with the Holy Spirit's wishes. Plead with him, reminding him of your needs, and keep praying earnestly for all Christians everywhere."

—**Ephesians 6:18 TLB**

A PAGE FROM THE PLAYBOOK

"As parents, we have a lot to pray about. Praying for our children is one of our greatest responsibilities. What an awesome thought to know that God hears and answers our prayers! '...Heavenly Father, teach me the importance of prayer that I may pass that knowledge to my children. As I tell You my deepest thoughts, fears, and desires in prayer, allow me to hear Your voice speaking to me in return. May I find Your will for my life as I learn to listen to You. Amen.'"

—**Kim Boyce**[2]

(2) Simply put, prayer is talking and listening to God. It is *not* a once a month, once a week, or once a day practice. It's a lifestyle of ongoing communication and friendship with God.

(a) First Thessalonians 5:17, Luke 18:1, and Ephesians 6:18 confirm that we are to pray *always*. How can you make this more of a reality in your family?

_____

_____

_____

(b) *Read* these verses and identify five conditions of successful prayer.

2 Chronicles 7:14 ♦ Jeremiah 29:12,13 ♦ Mark 11:24,25 ♦ John 15:7 ♦ 1 John 3:22,23

_____

_____

_____

(c) *Read* these verses and identify four causes of **un**successful prayer.

Proverbs 1:24-33 ♦ Proverbs 21:13 ♦ Proverbs 28:9 ♦ James 4:3

_____

_____

_____

(3) Prayer is both an act of *humility* and an act of *faith*. It is humility because it says by our actions that we don't have all the answers or the power that we need; it is faith in that it shows by our actions that we believe God is real, He hears our prayers, and He answers them.

(a) *Read* Ephesians 2:18; 3:12 and Hebrews 4:15,16; 10:19-22. What gives you the right to go to God in prayer on behalf of your children as well as yourself and others?

_____

_____

_____

(b) According to Isaiah 59:1,2 and Psalm 66:18-20, what is the number one thing that will hinder God from hearing your prayers?

_____

_____

_____

(c) If something is separating you from God, there is only one thing to do—get it out in the open. *Write* out and hide in your heart the powerful prayer principle of 1 John 1:9.

1 JOHN 1:9

_____

_____

If God is showing you a sin you need to confess, do it now. Ask Him to forgive you and wash you clean. If you still have feelings of guilt or condemnation after you pray, it is the enemy trying to keep you from restored fellowship with God. Hold on to the truth of Romans 8:1 and John 3:17,18; receive His forgiveness and move on.

AGELESS ADVICE

"Day and night your hand of discipline was heavy on me. My strength evaporated like water in the summer heat. Finally, I confessed all my sins to you and stopped trying to hide my guilt. I said to myself, 'I will confess my rebellion to the Lord.' And *you forgave me!* All my guilt is gone. Therefore, let all the godly pray to you while there is still time, that they may not drown in the floodwaters of judgment."

—Psalm 32:4-6 NLT

A PAGE FROM THE PLAYBOOK

"Your role is to become an intercessor for your child. An intercessor is one who prays for someone and makes possible the ability of that person to respond to God. No one else on earth will ever pray for your child with the fervency and consistency that you will. What an awesome opportunity to powerfully affect your child's life for eternity."

—Stormie Omartian[3]

(4) All through our parenting, we experience ample opportunities to become anxious, worried, or fearful over what may or may not happen to our children. The moment we begin to feel fear, God wants us to **run to Him** in prayer—anytime, anywhere about anything.

(a) According to Philippians 4:6, what are your prayers of petition to include? Why do you think this is important when it comes to dealing with anxiety, worry, and fear?

_____

_____

_____

(b) Take a moment to reflect on past prayers you have prayed that God has answered—especially ones involving your kids. Jot down a brief synopsis of at least three of these situations.

ANSWERED PRAYER #1

_____

_____

ANSWERED PRAYER #2

_____

_____

ANSWERED PRAYER #3

_____

_____

_____

Look for opportunities to share these proofs that God hears and answers prayer with your children. Your faith and their faith will be strengthened!

TRUE STORY:

"GOD HEARS AND GOD ANSWERS"

My oldest son, Austin, was in his senior year. He was receiving a number of scholarship offers for academics and football. His team was leading the district, and he was leading the team in interceptions and fumble recoveries. As Austin and his team members headed to the playoffs, he and our entire family were elated at their success. Although it was truly a blessed year, it was not without challenges.

I remember during the second to last game of the regular season, he was making a tackle and was struck hard in the knee. I was in the stands when it happened; I didn't see him get hit. All I saw was him wincing in pain and hopping on one leg. He immediately went back to his position to get ready for the next play, but when he realized he couldn't put any weight on his leg, he waved to his coach for permission to come out of the game.

Suddenly, I remembered my days of playing football. To my amazement, I was injured in the same knee during the same year of high school. I quickly made my way out of the stands and jumped the fence to get to the sideline. The professional trainer who had looked at Austin told me, "His MCL is torn...gone...he's done." Knowing the power of words, I asked him to keep his comments to himself and not speak them to my son (see Chapter 2, *Harnessing the Power of Your Words*).

I began to *pray* silently, asking God to heal Austin and thanking Him for healing him. Meanwhile, Austin became despondent and worried. I told him, "It'll be okay. Don't worry." When we got home, we put ice and compression on his knee and elevated his leg. I continued to pray in my head, asking for God's help like never before. Then I felt impressed to pray for my son *out loud* so he could hear me. So I turned to him and said, "I believe God is going to heal you." I then put my hands on him and prayed for God to heal him.

I must be honest with you, I was a bit embarrassed. Austin is my oldest son, and we are very close. I didn't want him to think I was becoming super spiritual, weird, or think I was "uncool." Nevertheless, I prayed earnestly. I truly believe God healed him right then and there. By that night, the swelling was gone and there was no blood-bruising. We went to the doctor on Monday to have an MRI done. It showed only a strain and no one could believe it. One week later, Austin was running. I believe the sideline trainer was right: My son's MCL was torn, but God restored it completely!

I know the power of prayer is real and God blessed and healed my son's knee. I intervened for him in prayer, pushing away fears of what he might think of me, believing God's promises instead. God will hear you too when you pray for your kids to return to Him, be healed, and overcome all of life's challenges. Trust Him. He will come through!

AGELESS ADVICE

"The LORD says, 'I will rescue those who love me. I will protect those who trust in my name. When they call on me, *I will answer*; I will be with them in trouble. I will rescue and honor them.'"

—Psalm 91:14,15 NLT

(5) Are you experiencing a situation with your kids that is producing anxiety, worry or fear? God wants you to bring it to Him in prayer, asking for His help and thanking Him for the way He has helped you in the past. Briefly describe the biggest challenge you are currently facing with your children. Then, using a Bible concordance, find specific verses from God's Word that promise His help or deliverance.

MY DILEMMA

_____

_____

_____

_____

_____

_____

GOD'S PROMISES TO HELP ME AND MY CHILDREN

_____

_____

_____

_____

_____

_____

_____

AFTER MEDITATING ON THESE SCRIPTURES, I FEEL GOD IS INSTRUCTING ME TO...

_____

_____

_____

_____

_____

_____

_____

This activity of searching the Scriptures for God's promises to overcome your problems can and should be applied to every challenging situation you face. There's nothing more powerful than praying God's Word. So write His promises down and speak them out!

A PAGE FROM THE PLAYBOOK

"Praying for your child is an awesome privilege. Have you ever considered praying for your child's future spouse? Depending on the age of your child, it could be a person they have yet to meet, or even someone who will be born in the future. ...Prayer for your child can include prayer for every aspect of his life. In fact, there is absolutely nothing that we cannot discuss with God. He is interested in every condition of your life and the life of your child. He, as our heavenly parent, is even more interested than we are in helping his kids make good choices."

Kendra Smiley[4]

AGELESS ADVICE

"...You who [are His servants and by your prayers] put the Lord in remembrance [of His promises], keep not silence."
—Isaiah 62:6 AMP

(6) God gives us a powerful instruction in Isaiah 62:6. He says we are to "put Him in remembrance of His promises." In other words, we are to *respectfully* remind Him of what He has said He will do for us in His Word. You know...like when your kids remind you of what you said you would do for them after they did what you asked.

(a) How reliable is God's Word—can you trust Him to do what He says? Carefully read these Scriptures and write what they mean to you.

Numbers 23:19 ♦ 2 Samuel 7:28 ♦ 1 Kings 8:56 ♦
Psalm 18:30; 119:140 ♦ Matthew 5:18

(b) What does God say in Jeremiah 1:12 that He does with His Word? What does this mean to you personally?

_____

_____

_____

(c) What does Psalm 103:20 say angels do when they hear God's Word? What does this mean to you?

_____

_____

_____

AGELESS ADVICE

"Bless the Lord, you His angels, mighty in strength, who perform His word, obeying the voice of His word!"

—Psalm 103:20 NASB

(7) Angels are real. They have a track record of reliability all through Scripture. Even though we can't see them, they are all around us—ready, willing, and able to help.

(a) According to Hebrews 1:14, what is one of the primary jobs of angels?

_____

_____

_____

(b) _Read_ Psalm 34:7; 91:11,12. Using these verses, write a prayer for your children, asking God for His angels to protect and guide them. This type of prayer is timeless and can be prayed on a regular basis.

MY PRAYER FOR ANGELIC PROTECTION & GUIDANCE

_____

_____

_____

_____

_____

_____

Check out these inspiring stories of angelic intervention to build your faith: Exodus 14:19; 2 Kings 6:8-22; Daniel 6:22; Matthew 1:18-24; 2:13-21; Luke 22:39-43; Acts 12:7-11.

AGELESS ADVICE

"...God is strong, and he wants you strong. So take everything the Master has set out for you, well-made weapons of the best materials. And put them to use so you will be able to stand up to everything the Devil throws your way. This is no afternoon athletic contest that we'll walk away from and forget about in a couple of hours. This is for keeps, a life-or-death fight to the finish against the Devil and all his angels."
—Ephesians 6:10-12 The Message

(8)   One thing that is very important to know about prayer is that it is one of the greatest weapons God has given us to protect and defend our children and family against the enemy (see Ephesians 6:10-18).

(a) According to 2 Corinthians 10:3,4 and Ephesians 6:12, what kind of battle are we in and who are we really fighting against when we run into problems?

_____

_____

_____

(b) *Write* out and commit to memory the incredible promise Jesus gives in Luke 10:19.

LUKE 10:19

_____

_____

_____

This promise holds true for you and your children. Also check out Mark 16:17; James 4:7; 1 Peter 5:8,9.

(c) Do you believe what Jesus says in Luke 10:19? Why or why not? Why is this promise important to your prayer life?

_____

_____

_____

AGELESS ADVICE

"This is what I want you to do: Ask the Father for whatever is in keeping with the things I've revealed to you. Ask in my name, according to my will, and he'll most certainly give it to you. Your joy will be a river overflowing its banks!"
—John 16:23.24 The Message

(9) Without question, *prayer is powerful!* Through faith in God's Word, prayer makes the impossible possible and turns dreams into reality. The question is, what are you praying and asking God to do for you and your children?

(a) *Read* God's promise to you and your children in Ephesians 3:20,21. What do these verses say to you? Do you believe it? Why or why not?

"Now to Him who is able to do exceedingly abundantly above all that we ask or think, according to the power that works in us, to Him be glory in the church by Christ Jesus to all generations, forever and ever. Amen."

—Ephesians 3:20,21 NKJV

_____

_____

_____

(b) *Read* God's promise to you and your children in James 5:16-18. What does this passage say to you? Do you believe it? Why or why not?

"...The earnest prayer of a righteous person has great power and produces wonderful results. Elijah was as human as we are, and yet when he prayed earnestly that no rain would fall, none fell for three and a half years! Then, when he prayed again, the sky sent down rain and the earth began to yield its crops."

—James 5:16-18 NLT

_____

_____

_____

(c) How have these verses and this lesson on prayer changed the way you look at prayer?

_____

_____

_____

SOMETHING TO THINK ABOUT

Darlene Deibler Rose, missionary to New Guinea, was imprisoned in a Japanese concentration camp during World War II. The food she was given was scant and loathsome. One day, looking out her cell window, she saw a distant bunch of bananas. Instantly, she craved the bite of banana. Everything inside her wanted one. She could smell and taste them. Dropping to her knees, she prayed, "Lord, I'm not asking you for a whole bunch.... I just want one banana. Lord, just one banana."

Then she began to rationalize. How could God get a banana through prison walls? "There was more of a chance of the moon falling out of the sky than of one of [the guards] bringing me a banana," she realized. Bowing again, she prayed, "Lord, there's no one here who could get a banana to me. There's no way for You to do it. Please don't think I'm not thankful for the rice porridge. It's just that—well, those bananas looked so delicious!"

The next morning, she heard the guard coming down the concrete walkway. It was the warden of the POW camp who had taken kindly to her. He looked at her emaciated body and, without saying a word, turned and left, locking the door behind him. Sometime later, another set of footsteps echoed down the walkway. The key turned and the door opened. The guard threw a huge yellow bundle into the cell, saying, "They're yours!" She counted them. It was a bundle of 92 bananas!

As she began peeling her bananas, Ephesians 3:20 came to her mind, and she never afterward read that verse without thinking of bananas.[5]

A PAGE FROM THE PLAYBOOK

"How do you pray for your child when you are unaware of all the specifics in his life? You can simply ask God to help him do the next right thing, whatever that may be. You see, if your child or mine will do the next right thing and follow that with the *next* right thing and then do the NEXT right thing, they will definitely be on the right track."

—**Kendra Smiley**[6]

(10) The list of ways you can pray for your children is *endless*. The fact is, you can take virtually every verse of Scripture and turn it into a prayer for your children. Here are seven specific things you can pray for them that are all based on the truth of God's Word. *Read* the verses and write a brief prayer for your children. An example has been given.

PRAY FOR...

SCRIPTURAL FOUNDATION

An intimate relationship with God.

Genesis 5:22-24 ♦ Isaiah 26:9 ♦
Psalm 27:4 ♦ Philippians 3:8,9

"Lord, I pray that child's name will have a firsthand relationship with You; that child's name will walk with You and be as close to You as Enoch was. Lord, may being in relationship with You be the one thing that drives and influences child's name life; may every other endeavor pale in comparison to knowing You and living righteously. In Jesus' name, Amen.

Divine connections with godly friends.

Proverbs 13:20; 27:17 ♦ 1 Corinthians 15:33

157

_____

_____

<u>Wisdom to make godly choices.</u>

Psalm 25:4,5, 9, 12; 48:14 ♦
John 16:13 ♦ James 1:5

_____

_____

_____

<u>Desire and discipline to keep himself/herself sexually pure.</u>

Job 31:1 ♦ Psalm 119:9 ♦ Proverbs 5:3-8 ♦ Ephesians 5:3
1 Corinthians 6:18 ♦ 1Thessalonians 4:3-7

_____

_____

_____

<u>Great favor and blessings with God and man.</u>

Genesis 6:8,9 ♦ Psalm 5:12 ♦ Proverbs 3:3,4

_____

_____

_____

<u>A godly spouse to spend his/her life with.</u>

Proverbs 5:18,19; 18:22 ♦ 2 Corinthians 6:14

_____

_____

_____

<u>A healthy, reverential fear of the Lord.</u>

Psalm 111:10 ♦ Proverbs 1:7; 10:27; 14:26,27

_____

_____

_____

What are your greatest desires and concerns for each of your children? Find out what God has to say about it in His Word, and then take it to Him in prayer. As you continue to read and study Scripture and come across powerful principles and promises, begin to write them down and make personalized prayers and proclamations out of them for your children and yourself.

AGELESS ADVICE

"Praise the LORD! How joyful are those who fear the Lord and delight in obeying his commands. Their children will be successful everywhere; an entire generation of godly people will be blessed."

—Psalm 112:1,2 NLT

A Page from the Playbook

"God answers the prayers of godly parents who want to raise godly children. Parents who spend time praying *for* their children, and praying *with* their children, demonstrate the importance of prayer. And they establish the right kind of pattern for their children. ...As you pray together as a family, you will be developing a family unity that no problems or storms later on can destroy. As you pray, you will all be focusing your attention in the same direction toward God who wants to bless His children, especially the family unit, more than you could ever imagine."

—**Charles Stanley**[7]

(11) There is only one thing better than praying for your kids and that is teaching them how to pray. By helping them personally discover the power of prayer and the vital role it plays in their lives, you are establishing a lifelong lifeline with the Creator of heaven and earth—a relationship that will carry them through everything they do.

(a) How did you learn how to pray? Is this something you can help your children learn to do?

_____

_____

_____

(b) One of the best ways to teach your children how to pray is to pray with them. Do you have a regular family prayer time? If so, when? If not, pray and ask the Lord what would be a good time for your family to pray together.

_____

_____

_____

Journal Your Journey! Gather your children together and ask each of them to tell you about prayers that God has answered. Get a journal or notebook and begin making a written history of the times God answers your prayers. Include the prayer request, the date, and a brief description of how God came through for you and your children. This is something you can also encourage your children to do on their own.

SENSEI SAYS...

"Parenting is a lifelong process. In some respects, it has no end. As our kids grow, our role and responsibility as their parents changes. Our job becomes more focused on encouraging and reminding them that they have the tools they need to be a success; it's their turn to choose what they feel is best."

—Mike Storms

Time to Reflect

When something disappointing or difficult happens to you or your children, don't make prayer your last resort—make it your *first response*. Are there destructive behavior patterns in your family line, such as alcoholism, lying, divorce, gluttony, or addiction to pornography that you don't want to see repeated in your children? PRAY. Are there negative, ungodly character traits in the lives of your children that you want to see replaced with positive, godly ones? PRAY. Search the Scriptures, secure God's promises that are yours through Christ, and pray a personalized prayer from the Word over them. Get God involved in every aspect of your life, and watch the wonderful things He brings about!

A PAGE FROM THE PLAYBOOK

"Even though you may not have been the best parent, even though you do not feel you were successful because you were just trying to survive, and even though you feel you can have no further influence on your children, you can still affect their lives through prayer. Your prayers could well be the key to unlocking years of rebellion and resentment."
—Stephen Arterburn & Jim Burns[8]

As you come to the end of this study, take time to reflect upon the things God is showing you. Write down any scriptures that jumped off the page and any principles that struck a chord in you.

_____

_____

_____

_____

_____

_____

_____

_____

_____

_____

_____

_____

_____

_____

_____

_____

_____

(1) *365 Day Brighteners Celebrating Mothers* (Siloam Springs, AR: Garborg's®, A brand of Dayspring® Cards, Inc., 2005) March 12; February 8. (2) See note 1, October 18; December 16. (3) Stormie Omartian, *The Power of a Praying Parent, Prayer and Study Guide* (Eugene, OR: Harvest House Publishers, 2000) p. 10. (4) Kendra Smiley, *Helping Your Kids Make Good Choices* (Ann Arbor, MI: Vine Books, an imprint of Servant Publications, 2000) p. 175. (5) Robert J. Morgan, *Nelson's Annual Preacher's Sourcebook—2002 Edition* (Nashville, TN: Thomas Nelson Publishers, 2001) p. 254. (6) See note 4, p. 173. (7) Charles Stanley, *How to Keep Your Kids on Your Team* (Nashville, TN: Thomas Nelson Publishers, 1986) pp.109-110, 129. (8) Stephen Arterburn and Jim Burns, *Parents Guide to Top Ten Dangers Teens Face* (Wheaton, IL: Tyndale House Publishers,1995) p. 316.

Appendix A

Healthy Media Menu Options

Toddler to Preteen

Cedarmont Kids Music (CDs & DVDs)

Cherub Wings—Sunny-Side-Up Entertainment (DVD series)

Gigi (DVD series and books)

Hermie & Friends by Max Lucado (DVD series & books)

Kids' Ten Commandments—TLC Entertainment (DVD series)

Miss Patty Cake—Integrity Music (DVD series)

The Donut Man (DVD series)

Veggie Tales (DVD series & books)

What's in the Bible? (DVD series)

Preteen to Young Adult

A Life of Faith Collection (books for girls)

Anne of Avonlea (book series)

Answers in Genesis (creation DVDs, books, magazines)

Adventures in Odyssey (audio theater)

Feature Films for Families (various movies)

Left Behind Kids (book series)

Sherwood Pictures (various Movies)

The Case for Christ, Faith, Creator by Lee Strobel (book series)

The Chronicles of Narnia (book series)

Secular Options for Consideration

Little House on the Prairie (DVD series & books)

The Waltons (DVD series) (teen)

Andy Griffith (DVD series) (teen)

Andrew Clements Books (preteen)

Popular Mechanics for Kids (DVD series)

The American Girl (DVD series)

You can check out many of these resources and others like them at your church library and the public library. Other options include borrowing some from a friend or purchasing them for your own lending library. A great place to check for value pricing and selection is Christian Book Distributors (www.cbd.com)

Appendix B

Suggested Reading

The Blessing, by Gary Smalley and John Trent, Ph.D. (New York, NY: Pocket Books, a division of Simon & Schuster, Inc., 1986).

Bringing Up Boys, by Dr. James Dobson (Wheaton, IL: Tyndale House Publishers, Inc., 2001).

Bringing Up Girls, by Dr. James Dobson (Wheaton, IL: Tyndale House Publishers, Inc., 2010).

Creative Correction, by Lisa Whelchel (Wheaton, IL: Tyndale House Publishers, Inc., 2005).

The New Dare to Discipline, by Dr. James C. Dobson (Wheaton, IL: Tyndale House Publishers, Inc., 1992).

Everyday Graces—A Child's Book of Manners, by Karen Santorum (Wilmington, DE: ISI Books, 2005).

Every Day I Pray for My Teenager, by Eastman Curtis (Lake Mary, FL: Charisma House, 1996).

Faithful Parents, Faithful Kids, by Greg Johnson and Mike Yorkey (Wheaton, IL: Tyndale House Publishers, Inc., 1993).

How to Keep Your Kids on Your Team, by Charles Stanley (Nashville, TN: Oliver-Nelson Books, a division of Thomas Nelson, Inc. Publishers, 1986).

The Key to Your Child's Heart, by Gary Smalley (Dallas, TX: Word Publishing, 1992).

The Language of Love, by Gary Smalley and John Trent, Ph.D. (Pomona, CA: Focus on the Family Publishing, 1988).

Parents Guide to Top Ten Dangers Teens Face, by Stephen Arterburn and Jim Burns (Wheaton, IL: Tyndale House Publishers, 1995).

The Power of a Parent's Words, by H. Norman Wright (Ventura, CA: Regal Books, a division of GL Publications, 1991).

The Power of a Praying Parent, by Stormie Omartian (Eugene, OR: Harvest House Publishers, 2007).

The Power of Praying for Your Adult Children, by Stormie Omartian (Eugene, OR: Harvest House Publishers, 2009).

Preparing for Adolescence, by Dr. James C. Dobson (Ventura, CA: Gospel Light, 2006).

Solid Answers, by Dr. James Dobson (Wheaton, IL: Tyndale House Publishers, Inc., 1997).

Teenagers—Parental Guidance Suggested, by Rich Wilkerson (Eugene, OR: Harvest House Publishers, 1983).

Venturing Into a Child's World, by Dr. Richard Dobbins (Old Tappan, NJ: Fleming H. Revell Company, 1985).

What the Bible Says About Child Training, by J. Richard Fugate (Apache Junction, AZ: Foundation for Biblical Research, 1996).

How Can You Have a Personal Relationship with God?

Throughout our journey to become better parents, I have frequently talked about the importance of turning to God for help. It is only through a personal relationship Him that you will have the ability to be a great parent and raise great kids. Without Him in your life, you cannot help connect your kids to God and establish a good spiritual foundation in their lives. Without Him, you are left to raise your children in your own strength and wisdom. The truth is, without Him you and I can do nothing.[1]

"Well, Mike, how can I have a personal relationship with God?" That's a good question. The answer is simple—**invite Him in**. He loves you and I so much He sent His Son, Jesus, to take our punishment for all the wrong we would ever do.[2] Jesus was perfect, without sin, and He died that our relationship with God might be restored.[3] When you *believe* and declare that Jesus Christ was God's Son, He lived a sinless life, died to pay for your sins, and rose from the grave to give you power to live right, you are born into His family.[4] Your relationship with Him is restored and His Spirit comes to live in your heart.[5]

Are you ready to invite God in? Then pray this simple prayer aloud from your heart:

God, I come to you just as I am. I know I have done many things wrong. I am sorry for my sins. Please forgive me and wash me clean on the inside with the life-giving blood of Jesus.[6] Come and live in my heart. Give me wisdom and strength to be a godly parent and live a life that pleases You.[7] I don't understand everything about being born into Your family, but I know I need You. Thank You for loving me and sending Jesus to die in my place and pay the penalty for my sin. Thank You for forgiving me and coming into my heart and showing me how to live. In His Name I pray, Amen.

If you prayed that prayer, you are now a child of God! Welcome to the family! The angels in heaven are standing and cheering at what you just did.[8] God loves you so much and is now living in your heart. You have access to everything you need to grow and mature into an all-star parent.[9]

Is there a friend or family member you know who has a relationship with God? Give them a call and tell them about your decision for God. You will excite them beyond words. We would also love to hear from you. Shoot us an email at mikestorms101@gmail.com _____.

We want to celebrate with you and help you get started in your new Christian life.

Scriptures for Personal Study:

(1) See John 15:5. (2) See John 3:16,17. (3) See 2 Corinthians 5:21; Hebrews 4:14-16. (4) See Romans 10:9,10. (5) See John 14:23; 1 John 3:24. (6) See 1 John 1:9. (7) See James 1:5; Psalm 32:8. (8) See Luke 15:10. (9) See 2 Peter 2:3.

Name:_____

Spouse Name:_____

Address:_____

Phone:_____

Kids Names:_____

Prayer Request:_____

Week 1:_____

CPSIA information can be obtained at www.ICGtesting.com
Printed in the USA
LVOW10s0305180614

390457LV00001B/2/P